YEADON'S REGISTER

of

L N E R

LOCOMOTIVES

Volume Nineteen

**Class D1, D2, D3 & D4,
& The M&GN 4-4-0's**

i

Copyright Booklaw/Railbus 2001
ISBN 1 899624 47 3

YEADON'S REGISTER OF L.N.E.R. LOCOMOTIVES - VOLUME 19

EDITOR'S NOTE & ACKNOWLEDGEMENTS

The 4-4-0's of the Great Northern Railway and Midland & Great Northern Railway feature in this the nineteenth volume of Yeadon's Register. The former GN engines made up the LNER's classes D1 to D4 whilst those inherited from the M&GN take-over in 1936, formed Class A Rebuild and classes D52 to D54.

The GN engines fared much better than those of the erstwhile M&GN but ironically photographs of the D4 class engines are sadly lacking within the collection and only one appears within this volume alas not in LNER livery but nevertheless a good photograph at that.

It will be seen that photographic coverage in general is excellent with virtually every change which occured to the GN engines illustrated. Likewise the M&GN coverage is good considering the short lived LNER careers of most M&GN engines. Altogether there are more than 220 illustrations covering the eight classes of engines listed within this particular Register. A feast indeed for those whose want is photographic evidence of detail change.

Volume 10 saw the first of the LNER 4-4-0's (D49's) highlighted by this series whilst Volume 14 featured the GER 4-4-0s (D13-D16) and joining them we now have eight more 4-4-0 classes. As you are well aware, there are many more to come, not least the GC engines which were to have been joining the GN classes in this volume but, because of space considerations, those particular 4-4-0's will appear in a later volume along with their larger 4-6-0 stablemates. However, for all those who were disappointed by the none appearance of the 'Directors' and their forebares we hope that the inclusion of the M&GN engines will make up for the 'delay'.

Eric Fry has once again been able to hold the reigns of enthusiasm whilst imparting his superb knowledge to the one or two 'grey' areas which crop up now and again during the production stages of this series. His proof reading abilities have ensured that you the reader get what WBY wanted - the true facts and figures as laid out in the original material compiled by WBY.

Brian Dyson and his archive staff at the University of Hull have again been ready to fulfil those last minute requests which, as they well know, keeps the series ticking over between serious bouts of typesetting.

Annie, Jean and Simon - thanks. We hope that you continue to support our endeavour to get this series finished. Hopefully this, the nineteenth volume of *Yeadon's Register of LNER Locomotives*, will meet your usual gracious approval.

And, once again, not forgetting you the reader, for your continuing support. Keep at it, there are more to come.

The next Register, Volume 20, will feature classes Q1 to Q4 and the LNER Q1 tank class.

The Yeadon Collection is available for inspection and anyone who wishes to inspect it should contact:-
The Archivist
Brynmor Jones Library
University of Hull
Hull
HU6 7RX
Tel: 01482-465265
A catalogue of the Yeadon collection is available.

First published in the United Kingdom by
BOOKLAW/RAILBUS 2001 in association with CHALLENGER
382 Carlton Hill, Nottingham NG4 1JA
www.booklawpublications.co.uk
www.booklawpublications.co.com

Printed and bound by The Amadeus Press, Cleckheaton.

INTRODUCTION

The locomotives featured in this volume were all 4-4-0's and came from two different companies; one was a constituent of the LNER, the Great Northern Railway, the other, the Midland & Great Northern Railway was a latecomer to the realms of the LNER and its locomotives were different from the GN examples being inclined towards Midland Railway design and outline.

The Great Northern engines comprised four classes D1, D2, D3 and D4, the latter comprising just six engines at Grouping and these were all rebuilt to D3 standard by 1928. Many of these 4-4-0's, though built before 1900 went on to serve the LNER until after the Second World War being used all over the system including the former North British lines in Scotland. They were of simple construction with two inside cylinders and it was perhaps this fact alone that saw to their longevity.

The M&GN engines on the other hand had fairly short working lives on the LNER. Almost immediately after, and within the following six months of the take-over on 1st October 1936 of their parent system by the LNER, many of the M&GN engines were withdrawn. There were a number of reasons for this not least was the fact that they were non-standard and also that each of the four classes actually added to LNER stock comprised smaller numbers of engines compared to their GNR counterparts.

The entire M&GN stock of locomotives was put straight onto the duplicate list, indicated by the time-honoured Stratford method of prefixing the existing engine number with a cypher.

Of the M&GN engines that got past the mass withdrawals of 1937, none left the East Anglian line to work anywhere else on the LNER excepting trips to Stratford works for repair or scrapping. By January 1945 they were all gone; perhaps W.W.II extending their lives beyond what was envisaged in 1936.

Class D1

Fifteen engines, all built in 1911, comprised Class D1. These were the last of the Ivatt 4-4-0's built for the GNR and were improvements on his earlier 4-4-0's which had been built at Doncaster from 1896 onwards to form basically four classes.

Numbered 51 to 65, these fifteen were all superheated from the start and differed outwardly from the previous batch of 4-4-0 ('1321' class/LNER D2) in having higher pitched boilers and bogies which extended further forward; piston valves replaced the usual slide valves.

During his period in office, Gresley had, in 1914, decided to introduce a larger 4-4-0 but this did not materialise and so the Ivatt examples were the only 4-4-0's to work on the GNR.

With the appearance of the first of the Atlantic types in 1898, the GN earlier 4-4-0's had little time working the principal express passenger trains on the main line and from thereon were gradually relegated to secondary passenger trains and mixed traffic duties, though they often double-headed to work the heavier express trains. The D1's themselves were never intended to work main line express trains but were often called upon to do so.

In 1925, after being suitably altered to the North British Section load gauge, the whole class was transferred to the Scottish Area being fitted with Westinghouse braking gear at

Cowlairs. The vacuum ejector was retained for alternative train braking.

Although the rest of the class were built with Ramsbottom type safety valves, Nos.60 and 61 were fitted with Ross 'pop' valves, the first GN engines so fitted. A special seating was required on their boilers which had initially been drilled to accept the Ramsbottom valves.

Three of the 1911 built boilers were still in use at the withdrawal of 2205 (11/48), 62208 (7/50) and 62215 (2/50); the first two still fitted with Ramsbottom safety valves. The latter engine also kept its original Schmidt type superheater to withdrawal along with No.2209. Seven of the engines sent back to the Southern Area from Scotland in 1930-32, Nos.3052, 3053, 3055, 3056, 3059, 3060 and 3062, retained their Ramsbottom safety valves for a time but all were later fitted with 'pops'. Also, during the period 1932 to 1934, their superheaters were changed from Schmidt to Robinson type which could be discerned by the addition of a circular access cover.

The standard lubrication was a Wakefield mechanical type, placed on the right hand running plate, for cylinders and valves with syphon type for the coupled axleboxes. In 1924 No.3056 had its Wakefield replaced by a sight feed lubricator on the left inside the cab, with the pipes enclosed in a sheet metal cover to where they branched off to the four feed points; 3056 kept this method of lubrication until withdrawal (*see* photo 27 on page XX). Another, though unrecorded, variant of lubrication was affixed to No.3052 at a Doncaster repair in November 1932 when the Wakefield was changed for a Hulburd mechanical type; the Wakefield was later restored to No.3052.

Five of the seven which returned to Southern Area lost their Westinghouse equipment in 1937, the other two, Nos.3053 and 3059 kept theirs until 1939 and 1942 respectively. In the interim period after return from Scotland the seven were stored at Doncaster and then went to work on the former Great Eastern lines where the Westinghouse brake was at times useful. Six of the eight engines still resident in Scotland kept their Westinghouse gear until well into the Second World War period when they were altered to steam brake. Nos.3051 and 3061 kept their Westinghouse brake to withdrawal.

Livery during the GN period was the standard passenger green with lining. After 1923 this livery was retained although to the LNER version of green. From 1928 black with red lining became the norm and from 1929 numbers were transferred from tenders to cab sides.

From the start of their sojourn in Scotland, Cowlairs became responsible for their maintenance with boilers sent from Doncaster when required. The seven which returned to Southern Area reverted to Doncaster maintenance.

For most of their working lives the D1's worked in areas well away from former GN lines being allocated at the end of hostilities in 1945 as far north as Perth and on ex-M&GN lines where they did some good work during the war period and thereafter. Only 62203 ended its life at a former GN shed, having nine months at Colwick before withdrawal in August 1950.

Withdrawals started in 1946 when five engines were scrapped still with their 3000 numbers. The other ten survived long enough to gain the numbers allocated to the class in the 1943 renumbering scheme. Seven engines lasted into BR days but only three, 62203 in England and 62208 and 62215 in

D1 - Fifteen engines, 51 to 65, were built March to July 1911 of which thirteen had Ramsbottom safety valves. Note the anti-vacuum valve at the base of the smokebox. Painting is shop grey. All fifteen engines had a 3ft 1in. deep cab side cut out.

D2 - Five engines Nos.1321 to 1325 were built in 1898. This shows No.1321 as running at Grouping. Note the straight running plate and extra casing over the coupling rod which applied only to these five and one later rebuild. The coupling rod has already been changed to a fluted type.

D3 - In November 1912 a start was made on putting a 4ft 8in. instead of 4ft 2in. boiler on to Ivatt's first 4-4-0 engines. No.1359 was the first one and it was fitted with a 2ft 2¼in. chimney.

Scotland, got the 60,000 addition to their numbers. The last D1, No.2209 from Stirling shed, was withdrawn in November 1950 making the class extinct.

Class D2

This was the largest class of former GNR 4-4-0's on the LNER numbering seventy at Grouping with two more added shortly afterwards by rebuilding from Class D3 (Nos.1305ₙ and 4320). Built in seven lots between 1898 and 1909, these were also designated class D1 on the Great Northern but were distinguished from the 1911 engines by also being known as '1321' class engines. Designated running numbers in order of building was: 1321 to 1340, 1361 to 1399, 1180, and 41 to 50.

These engines were a further development of Ivatt's '400' class and had larger boilers and (after the first five, 1321 to 1325) longer smokeboxes and frames some six inches longer, though before the third lot (1336 to 1340 and 1361 to 1365) were being built in 1899 a further batch of ten '400's appeared followed by another batch of ten soon afterwards.

The first five soon received the longer smokeboxes though retained the horizontal running plate with separate casing over the coupling rods similar to the '400' class. The other sixty-five had the running plate raised to clear the coupling rods.

One engine, No.1381, was fitted with a Robinson superheater in 1914 and the chimney and blastpipe were moved further forward to accommodate the header. A further twenty-three were superheated after Grouping, during the period 1928 to 1930 (eight) and then fifteen during 1935 to 1937, all with Robinson type which required a 9¾in. longer smokebox. Prior to the 1914 fitting by Gresley, Ivatt had tried a Baldwin smokebox superheater on No.1383 in February 1910; this appliance required the smokebox to be extended a further 2ft. 2½in. forward though with chimney and blastpipe kept in the same position. In April 1914 this arrangement was taken off and 1383 reverted to a normal smokebox. Another engine, No.1369, was fitted with Ivatt's U-tube superheater in February 1911; this superheater did not require an extension to the smokebox but only lasted until January 1915.

In 1928 many saturated Diagram 7 boilers carried by the D2's (also used on classes D1, J1, J2, J5, J6, N1 and N2) were condemned and the affected engines spent up to six months in works awaiting new boilers. As a crisis measure ten superheated boilers were converted to saturated and fitted to the D2's. Three D2's had been fitted with superheated boilers in the early part of the year. In November 1929 three further engines received superheated boilers, followed by two more in 1930.

The D2's were originally fitted with Ramsbottom safety valves but all except seven gained the Ross 'pop' type when fitted with newer boilers, although some of those later reverted to Ramsbottom when fitted with an older boiler.

It will be noted in the tables that many D2's (and indeed other GN 4-4-0's) spent longer periods in works than was usual. This resulted from the fact that arc welding was required for the cracks caused by weakness in the frames around the horn blocks; a constant fault inspected daily at shed.

From October 1924 onwards, a number of the class had their chimneys reduced in height so that they could work trains from the GN Section to seaside towns on the GE Section. King's Cross shed started the ball rolling by fitting J6 type chimneys to Nos.3041, 3042, 3049 and 4336. These were followed by Doncaster works dealing with No.4377 and No.4372 in early 1926. The latter was shedded at York at the time but moved south to Sheffield in May until October 1927. No.4377 got a

chimney similar to those fitted on the 0-8-0 and 0-8-2T engines. In the mid-1930's a number of those with tall chimneys had 1½in. turned off whilst during 1936/7 others got the J6 chimney which enabled them to work onto the GE Section. From March 1939 all those survivors not so fitted received the J6 type chimney which then saw the whole class having unrestricted route clearance throughout the former GE territory. Lower dome covers of the D3 type had been fitted in many cases before Grouping but even lower domes giving a height above rail level to 12ft. 4⅞in. were fitted by King's Cross in 1924.

Whittaker tablet exchanging apparatus was fitted to the tenders of engines working on the former Midland & Great Northern Railway from 1936. Those known to have had this equipment fitted include: 3045, 3046, 4321, 4322, 4327, 4329, 4335, 4368, 4373, 4374, 4376, 4394.

The D2's were allocated the number series 2150 to 2201 in the 1943 scheme, Nos.4305 and 4320 the post-Grouping rebuilds from D3 being allocated the first two numbers. Only four of the survivors failed to gain the new numbers before withdrawal.

In GN days the whole class wore the standard GN passenger lined green livery and after Grouping gradually changed to LNER lined green. Like the D1 class, the D2's acquired black livery with red lining after the 1928 painting economies. W.W.II saw NE in place of LNER on the tender sides and the disappearance of the red lining. Of the thirty-one D2's which entered BR only one, 62172, got the 60,000 addition to its number, however, it did not receive a cast smokebox numberplate. Its tender was lettered BRITISH RAILWAYS, one of only two so done; the other being ᴇ2188.

Initially built for both main line and secondary duties, the D2's were often seen on main line workings usually double-heading Atlantics on the principal expresses but most of their work was done in Lincolnshire and Nottinghamshire in the early years, a trend which was to carry on throughout the LNER period too. They were basically 'maids of all work' and could be found heading fast fitted goods trains on the main line, express passenger trains, stopping passenger, unfitted goods and even branch line work. In GN days four of the class, Nos.1396, 1397, 1398 and 1399, were outstationed at Trafford Park for use on the fitted goods from Deansgate to King's Cross and the express from Manchester (Central) to Nottingham. They reappeared in the area in 1932-33 when five were sent there to work on the Cheshire Lines out of Trafford Park and Heaton Mersey sheds. Besides their long association with York, the D2's found other work in the North Eastern area; three ending their days at Hull Botanic shed after a long period in store at nearby Springhead works. Some sheds outside of the former GN territory such as Bury St Edmunds and Frodingham had a single example of D2 by the beginning of W.W.II, the four surviving sheds on the M&GN had nine between them; Boston had the largest allocation at ten engines whilst Colwick had eight. The others could be found at sheds along the East Coast Main Line and in Lincolnshire. W.W.II found plenty of work for the surviving D2's with none being withdrawn between 1940 and 1945.

Many D2's spent much of the 1930's stored at various periods, suitably tallowed, awaiting an upturn in traffic; one engine spent three years stored at Doncaster works before returning to traffic in 1933. In September 1936 the first of the class to be condemned, No.4334 superheated in 1928, was withdrawn. A further sixteen engines (four recently superheated) went to the scrapyard before the outbreak of war in September

1939 slowed down the rate of withdrawal. The last D2, No.62172 was not finally withdrawn until June 1951, nearly fifty-one years old.

Classes D3 and D4

Fifty one engines comprised GNR classes D3 and D2, all introduced by Ivatt, they were the first 4-4-0's operated by the Great Northern. The first engine, No.400, appeared in December 1896 and for six months was the only one of its kind on the GN until the second and third 4-4-0's came out in May the following year; these were followed by a further eight in June and a batch of ten in the final three months of 1897. Twenty more were put into traffic during 1898 and another ten during the final two months of the century.

These engines formed what was basically the later LNER class D4. However, during the Gresley GN period forty-five of the class were rebuilt to what became LNER Class D3 by the substitution of a new larger diameter 4ft 8in. boiler in place of the original of 4ft 2in. diameter. Having made a start with No.1359 in November 1912, most rebuilding was carried out before Grouping with the LNER finishing the job during the 1920's. The final engine to be rebuilt from D4 to D3 being No.4358 in June 1928.

The running plate was straight with a separate casing over the coupling rods, but No.1320 out new in June 1898 did not have the casing and the main running plate was instead raised in the vicinity of the coupled wheels to provide the necessary clearance for the side rods. This arrangement was adopted for the final ten engines, Nos.1351-1360, as it was also on the larger '1321' class (LNER D2) after the first five had been built.

The new boiler (Diagram 8) was pitched higher than the previous boiler and five inch shorter chimneys were fitted to the first six rebuilds, however, all the others, starting with No.1316 got taller chimneys. Superheating was ordered for some of these boilers in GN days but was cancelled; likewise during the LNER period superheating was again envisaged but was subsequently abandoned before any were so fitted.

Further to the six D4 becoming D3 after Grouping, two D3 were rebuilt to D2 standard in LNER days; No.4305 in October 1923 and 4320 in June 1926.

During 1930/31 seven of the class, then working in the Darlington area, were fitted with Raven fog signalling apparatus at Darlington works. They were 4075 (26/12/30), 4077 (5/8/31), 4347 (19/5/31), 4348 (28/10/30), 4349 (8/5/31), 4350 (7/10/31) and 4354 (24/12/30). The Raven F.S.A. was taken out of use at the end of October 1933 and the equipment removed from the engines. Most of the work carried out by these engines was on the Stainmore line to Penrith where the weather could be harsh during winter months and complaints from enginemen led to four (4075, 4077, 4349 and 4354) being altered at Doncaster during the first half of 1935 to give extra protection on the footplate. The actual alterations saw the cab roof extended back a further 8ins. whilst the rear edge of the cab side sheets was made straight without any cut-out. A single side window on each side was put in. The other four D3's working the line (the original seven were joined by No.4313 in March 1933) were transferred away before they were altered.

For working tender first on passenger trains, some were fitted during the 1930's with front end heater connection.

After the first six rebuilds, a chimney height of 2ft 7¼in. was standardised until March 1939. The six which got shorter chimney when re-boilered, were later fitted with the standard height chimney in most cases; No.4306 still retained its shorter

chimney acquired at rebuilding as late as May 1937. From 1931 some engines had 1½in. turned off the rim of their chimneys enabling them to work over certain parts of the former GE territory and in 1936-37 several had the 1ft 11¼in. high J6 type chimney fitted which gave them full access to all parts of the ex GE system. From March 1939 the surviving D3's were gradually fitted with J6 chimneys.

During World War Two, five Diagram 7 boilers were converted to Diagram 8, and these had inspection doors instead of washout plugs. Ramsbottom safety valves were standard for the class in GN days but a large proportion of them acquired Ross 'pop' valves as new boilers were supplied although eleven engines never got the 'pops' valves and some of those which did reverted back to Ramsbottom valves when they received an older boiler at shopping.

For use on the M&GN lines, at least eight, Nos.3400, 4306, 4310, 4315, 4319, 4345, 4352 and 4355, were fitted with the Whittaker tablet exchanging apparatus.

Intended for secondary line work, these 4-4-0's, like all the other similar GN types, were often called upon to work main line express passenger duties either singly, in pairs or double-heading single-wheelers or Atlantics. They were to be found at all the larger sheds on the ECML during GN days as well as the West Riding; Colwick had the largest allocation at thirteen in 1912 and sixteen in 1922, New England on the other hand rarely had use for them until 1936 when the M&GN was absorbed and the D3's became regular engines on that line. Only a few worked in rural Lincolnshire in GN days but by Grouping both Boston and Lincoln sheds had a dozen between them, four of which were the unrebuilt D4, the other two D4 being at Grantham. From Colwick they would work westwards to Derby, Burton and Stafford, south to Leicester and along the various GN branches north of Nottingham. Passenger, beer and milk traffic was their usual load. During the 1930's the LNER sent a number of them off to the North Eastern area were they worked from the smaller sheds at Barnard Castle, Middleton-in-Teesdale and Penrith; others were to be found at Botanic Gardens, Darlington, Kirkby Stephen, Selby, Starbeck and York. Even some GC Section sheds saw D3's allocated for short periods during the 1930's with Mexborough, Sheffield and Woodford having them for a few months or weeks at a time; just days in the case of No.4347 at Woodford. No.4309 was at Frodingham during May 1937 working local passenger traffic and was replaced by a D2. At the end of the LNER there were eleven at former GN sheds with Colwick maintaining the highest quota at six, three at ex GCR sheds and five at South Lynn on the M&GN.

All had standard GNR passenger green livery when taken over by the LNER. The last one to get the GNR painting, with two greens and scalloped corners to the lining panel, before Grouping was No.1346, which came out of Doncaster on 16th December 1922. However, it did not carry the company's initials on the tender. From late August 1923 to the end of January 1924, the area suffix N was added to the number and four D3's got this: 1348N (24/8/23), 1309N (22/9/23), 1352N (17/11/23) and 1349N (12/1/24). The next one ex works, No.4319 on 23rd February 1924, got the 1924 number with 3000 added. Green livery was still applied until black with red lining became standard after 1928 and from 1929 the numbers were transferred from tender to cab sides. No.4346 ran in green until its shopping of December 1932 and was the last GN 4-4-0 to do so.

In line with company wartime policy, the LNER on the tender was cut to NE from June 1942 and many of those

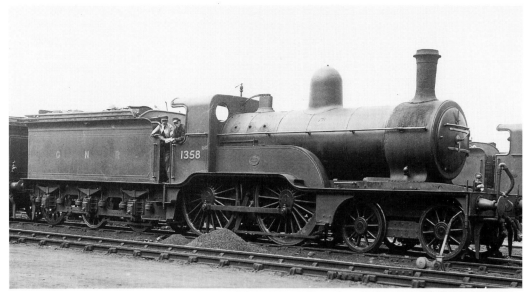

D4 - No.1358 in full GNR livery. One of the six D4's which entered the LNER and was the last one rebuilt to D3 standard.

M&GN Class A Rebuild - From the original fifteen built by Beyer, Peacock between 1882 and 1888, only five, Nos.23, 25, 26, 27 and 28, remained for the LNER to take over on 1st October 1936. These five had been rebuilt between 1895 and 1906, and again from November 1919 to March 1927. The small initials on the tender gradually gave place to 14in. LMS style from 1928.

D52 - At LNER take-over there were seventeen engines in the class, Nos.1, 3, 4, 5, 7, 11, 12, 13, 14, 17, 18, 37, 38, 42, 43, 47 and 48 which were substantially as built by Sharp, Stewart & Co. in 1894.

renumbered in 1946, usually at home sheds, still had those initials even though the full LNER had been restored from January 1946. Those renumbered by Doncaster works had the LNER restored in shaded transfers whilst stocks were available. The last to have this style was No.2144, out 22nd March 1947.

One engine, No.4075, was given special treatment in September 1944. Chosen to haul the Officer's saloons and special trains, it got fully lined green livery and the LNER coat of arms on the tender though only NE was applied. It was numbered No.1 to start with but was then given the number 2000, which was to be the first number in the group chosen for the 4-4-0 tender engines of the LNER. Later it got the LNER restored albeit in yellow unshaded Gill sans and then went on to have full BR numbering with emblem.

Withdrawals had started in 1935 but ceased two years later when fourteen engines had been scrapped. Only one was withdrawn during the war period such was the traffic requirements of the time. Allocated number block 2115 to 2148 in the 1943 renumbering scheme, the surviving D3's got their new numbers from 1946 onwards and all except 4073, 4312 and 4356 were renumbered. No.2000 was to have been 2119 but kept 2000 instead. Although nineteen D3's became BR property, only three survived long enough to have the addition of the BR 60,000 to their numbers: 62000, 62131 and 62135, the former being the last of the class when withdrawn in October 1951. No.2140 acquired the 'E' prefix and BRITISH RAILWAYS on its tender.

M&GN Class A - No LNER classification.

Only five of the original fifteen built by Beyer, Peacock between 1882 and 1888 survived to become LNER engines in October 1936. Numbered 23, 25, 26, 27 and 28, these five had all been rebuilt twice by the M&GN, once between 1895 and 1906 and again between 1919 and 1927.

All were alike in detail and each possessed a 3000 gallon tender of the Midland Railway type with 3 tons of coal.

Two, Nos.25 and 27, were given the 0 prefix to their numbers, which was carried out at Melton Constable in November 1936; the other three kept their brass numbers until withdrawal. The only one of the five to have LNER applied to its tender was No.025, this at a general repair at Stratford during early 1937 when it received a livery of black paint without lining.

The five were spread about the former M&GN system from Yarmouth to Peterborough and Melton to Spalding working both goods and passenger trains.

Withdrawals took place during 1936, 1937 and 1938 but the last one, No.025 was not withdrawn until May 1941. All were cut up at Stratford after a somewhat brief LNER career.

M&GN Class B - LNER D52

Seventeen engines built by Sharp, Stewart & Co. in 1894, and six built by Beyer, Peacock & Co. in 1899, comprised M&GN Class B at take-over in 1936 and these were basically as built. Designed by S.W. Johnson the Midland Railway C.M.E., the original class was some forty strong but rebuilding by the M&GN gradually saw divisions within the class and Class C (D53) and D (D54) were formed from the rebuilt engines.

Boilers were supplied by Derby which built new ones at first but during the 1930's began to supply second-hand boilers. None were ever superheated.

Ten of the twenty-three Class B engines were early withdrawals so did not get LNER numbering. However, this class comprised the largest of the ex M&GN 4-4-0's taken over by the LNER.

After their first overhauls at Stratford the survivors came out in plain black livery with no lining, which was then current LNER policy.

When LNER Class D52 was allotted on 28th July 1942, only five, Nos.011, 012, 038, 043 and 076 then survived. Nos.038 and 076 would have been allotted LNER numbers 2050 and 2051 in the general renumbering scheme of 1943 but did not survive long enough to appear on the finalised printed version of December 1943. The withdrawal of 038 on 27th September 1943 made the D52's extinct.

M&GN Class C - LNER D53

Between May 1929 and April 1931 seven M&GN Class B engines became Class C when given fresh boilers with Belpaire firebox, although otherwise of similar dimensions to the original round topped version. The cabs were also altered, which was an improvement on the previous design, giving better protection.

No.36 was the first Class C withdrawn but the others, Nos.2, 6, 44, 49, 50 and 77 all went on to gain LNER numbers and initials. Usually Melton Constable changed the numbers by removing the brass numbers on the cab sides and applying hand painted unshaded numbers with the prefix 0; the M&GN on the tenders was left intact until Stratford changed it to LNER with transfers. Engines changing numbers at Melton were; 02, 06, 050. Those not already having LNER numbers were changed at Stratford; again shaded transfers were used for that purpose. Unlined black paint was applied to all those receiving general repairs.

Like the D52 class engines, the D53 were 'maids of all work' on the M&GN and could be found at all the sheds on that system besides the Peterborough sheds at Spital Bridge (LMS) and New England; those allocated to the former Midland shed at Spital Bridge were transferred to the former Great Eastern shed at Peterborough East when the LNER became fully responsible for the M&GNR.

In the 1943 renumbering scheme, Nos.050, 06 and 077 were allotted LNER numbers 2052, 2053 and 2054 respectively but all three were withdrawn before the 1946 implementation. With the withdrawal of No.050 from Yarmouth Beach shed in January 1945, Class D53 then became extinct.

M&GN Class D - LNER D54

The M&GN were forever rebuilding their locomotives and Class D was typical of that trait. Three of the engines built by Sharp, Stewart in 1894 and seven they built in 1896 - all basically Class B engines - were later rebuilt with larger diameter boilers complete with Belpaire fireboxes although the first two rebuilds, Nos.39 and 55 carried a round-top version until brought into line in 1924 and 1925 respectively.

Chimneys varied not only between classes but also between individual engines within classes. The Derby influence was very evident throughout most of their lives as will be seen from the illustrations to be found later in this volume.

Tenders remained unchanged throughout in most cases but some had their coal capacity increased from 3 tons by the addition of an extra rail on each side of the tender. No.54 received the flush-sided 3000 gallon tender from Class A

Rebuild No.22 after that engine was withdrawn in 1936. All were fitted with Whittaker tablet exchanging apparatus but only on the nearside side of the tender, unlike Class D52 some of which had them on both sides.

Class D54 worked mainly express passenger trains on account of having a larger grate area than the other 4-4-0's as well as having greater adhesion weight. During LNER days the D54's were allocated to Melton Constable, South Lynn and Yarmouth Beach.

Plain black livery with no lining was worn by the those seven which managed to survive their first visit to Stratford. LNER was applied to the tender sides. Nos.055 and 056 were to have been renumbered 2055 and 2056 in the 1943 scheme but their demise before the list was printed in December 1943 saw them excluded.

Three D54's were withdrawn in the early purges: Nos.39 and 57 (both 2/37) and 45 (11/36). Five of the remaining seven lasted into 1943 when the class was rendered extinct by the withdrawal of No.055 on 5th November 1943 and 056 the previous day.

(below) **D53 - Between May 1929 and April 1931, seven Class B engines, Nos.2, 6, 36, 44, 49, 50 and 77, got boilers with a Belpaire type firebox, smokebox doors with dog clips and a cross rail, and a better cab. All were fitted with Ross 'pop' safety valves. No.36 was withdrawn from service 4th January 1937 but the others all got LNER numbers and initials.**

(below) **D54 - Three of the engines built in 1894 by Sharp, Stewart, Nos.39, 45 and 46, together with seven they built in 1896, Nos.51 to 57, were later rebuilt with larger diameter boiler. In 1909 No.45 was fitted with a MR G7 boiler with Belpaire firebox and extended smokebox. An extra coal rail was added to the tender. Between 1910 and 1916 seven more, Nos.46, 51 to 54, 56 and 57 were similarly rebuilt. Until 1928-30 they had yellow-brown paint, armorial on front splasher and small company initials on the tender. The class was completed by the addition of No.39 in January 1924 and No.55 in July 1925. Until around 1930, all ten had the Johnson type of smokebox door fastening by wheel and handle supplemented by three dog clips on the lower part of the door. The handrail was continuous with this type of door.**

The other two of the batch, Nos.60 and 61, had Ross 'Pop' safety valves on a mounting prepared for Ramsbottom type. This engine is fully painted and lined in GNR type livery. Note that the tender is a Stirling design with three coal rails, equal axle spacing, and wooden buffer beam.

The final engine, No.65 had anti-vacuum valve at base of the smokebox and also a steam cylinder for operating the damper of the draught retarder. This protection for the Schmidt superheater element was soon found to be unecessary. To accommodate the engine cylinders, a gap had to be cut in the frames and a thin cover plate was fixed over it.

Well before the LNER take-over, the anti-vacuum valves at the base of the smokebox had been removed, as a Gresley type on the centre of the superheater header proved a big improvement.

CLASS D 1

3051

Doncaster 1296.

To traffic 3/1911.

REPAIRS:
Don. 4/10—16/12/22.**G.**
Don. 30/10/24—5/2/25.**G.**
Cow. ?/?—16/7/26.**H.**
Westinghouse fitted.
Cow. ?/?—?/9/27.**G.**
Cow. ?/?—18/5/29.**G.**
Cow. ?/?—31/1031.**G.**
Cow. ?/?—26/10/35.**G.**
Cow. ?/?—20/4/37.**L.**
Cow. ?/?—10/3/42.**L.**
Cow. ?/?—26/9/42.**L.**
Cow. 13/3/43—3/4/43.**G.**
Cow. ?/?—26/9/43.**L.**
No heavy repair between 10/35
& 3/43 when it did only 51,902
miles. Stored 2/44 to 2/46.

BOILERS:
7062.
7171 16/12/22.
7091 *(ex3062)* 18/5/29.
7067 *(ex3064)* 31/10/31.
8810 *(new)* 26/10/35.
9133 *(ex3061)* 3/4/43.

SHEDS:
Copley Hill.
Haymarket 22/1/25.
Hawick 3/43.

RENUMBERED:
3051 5/2/25.
2202 allocated.

CONDEMNED: 15/2/46.

3052

Doncaster 1297.

To traffic 4/1911.

REPAIRS
Don. 17/12/21—18/3/22.**G.**
Don. 22/2—25/9/24.**G.**
Don. 14—22/1/25.**L.**
Cow. 11—15/5/25.**L**
Cow. 30/4—28/8/26.**G.**
Westinghouse fitted.
Water scoop removed.
Cow. 16/12/26—15/3/27.**H.**
Cow. 18/10—6/12/28.**G.**
Lined black.
Cow. 21—30/3/29.**L.**

Cow. 24/6—8/8/31.**G.**
Don. 23/9—3/11/32.**G.**
Don. 24/8—13/10/34.**G.**
Don. 9/2—28/3/26.**G.**
Don. 10—31/2/37.**L.**
Westinghouse to vacuum.
Don. 27/6—28/7/38.**G.**
Don. 31/8—14/10/41.**G.**
Don. 9/1—11/2/44.**G.**
Str. 24/1—24/2/46.**L.**
Don. 1/6—4/9/47.**G.**
Don. 13—25/3/48.**L.**
Stored: 4/11/32—15/6/33.
19/10/39—16/2/40.
9/3/40—1/4/41.
12/1/48—4/11/49.

BOILERS:
7063.
7162 25/9/24.
7740 13/10/34.
9132 28/7/38.
9780 4/9/47.

SHEDS:
Copley Hill.
Dunfermline 22/1/25.
Doncaster 26/7/32.
Ipswich 5/10/33.
Norwich 29/9/36.
Yarmouth 2/7/37.
Norwich 17/10/37.
Cambridge 26/5/40.
Norwich 15/5/41.
Yarmouth Beach 18/12/41.
Melton Constable 5/5/46.
Colwick 6/11/49.

RENUMBERED:
3052 25/9/24.
2203 13/1/47
62203 25/3/48

CONDEMNED: 31/8/50.
Cut up at Darlington.

3053

Doncaster 1298.

To traffic 4/1911

REPAIRS:
Don. 18/8—6/11/20.**G.**
Don. 20/3—23/6/23.**G.**
Don. 22/5—10/10/25.**G.**
Cow. ?/?—8/27.**G.**
Westinghouse fitted.
Cow. ?/?—1/11/30.**G.**
Cow. ?/?—4/12/30.**L.**
Don. 30/5/31.**L.**

Don. 26/8—14/10/33.**G.**
Don. 22/2—21/3/36.**G.**
Don. 22/5—12/6/37.**L.**
Engine brake reverted to vac.
Don. 19/2—12/3/38.**G.**
Don. 1/4—6/5/39.**G.**
Westinghouse removed.
Don. 2/9—28/10/39.**L.**
Don. 29/11—6/12/41.**L.**
Don. 26/6—17/7/43.**G.**

BOILERS:
7064.
7177 23/6/23.
7070 *(ex3058)* 1/11/30.
8939 21/3/36.
9056 17/7/43.

SHEDS:
Copley Hill
Cambridge 5/1/24.
Ladybank 10/11/25.
Haymarket 5/12/26.
Doncaster 23/12/30.
Norwich 9/6/31.
Peterborough East 25/5/32.
New England 14/9/32.
Boston 21/4/33.
Norwich 21/10/33.
Melton Constable 5/1/42.
Yarmouth Beach 13/8/45.

RENUMBERED:
2204 allocated.

CONDEMNED: 9/3/46.
Into Don. for cut up 22/3/46.

3054

Doncaster 1299.

To traffic 4/1911.

REPAIRS:
Don. 24/10—16/12/22.**L.**
Don. 11/1—23/8/24.**G.**
Don. 1/1—7/1/25.**L.**
Cow. ?/?—4/27.**G.**
Westinghouse fitted.
Cow. ?/?—21/2/31.**G.**
Cow. ?/?—16/5/31.**L.**
Cow. ?/?—24/3/34.**G.**
Cow. 25/3/34.**N/C.**
Cow. ?/?—13/10/39.**L.**
Cow. 31/8—5/10/40.**G.**
Cow. ?/?—30/1/43.**H.**
Cow. ?/?—13/1/44.**L.**
Westinghouse to steam brake.
Cow. ?/?—19/2/44.**L.**
Cow. 28/11—22/12/45.**G.**
Not in use for 237 days in 1944

and 156 days in 1945

BOILERS:
7065.
7064 *(ex3053)* 23/8/24.
7177 *(ex3053)* 21/2/31.
7062 *(ex3065)* 24/3/34.
7177 *(ex3063)* 5/10/40.
7063 *(ex3063)* 22/12/45.

SHEDS:
Copley Hill
Hawick 10/1/25.
Haymarket 13/5/27.
Polmont 5/3/30.
Haymarket 10/30.
Perth 9/41.
Dunfermline 28/10/47.

RENUMBERED:
3054 23/8/24.
2205 22/6/46

CONDEMNED: 8/11/48

3055

Doncaster 1300.

To traffic 4/1911.

REPAIRS:
Don. 24/11/19—7/2/20.**G.**
Don. 4/6—29/9/23.**G.**
Don. 31/3—25/7/25.**G.**
Cow. ?/?—31/7/27.**L.**
Westinghouse fitted.
Cowlairs data missing.
Cow. ?/?—13/8/32.**G.**
Don. 3/2—17/3/34.**G.**
Don. 28/12/35—18/1/36.**G.**
Don. 20—27/2/37.**L.**
Westinghouse to vacuum.
Don. 5—19/3/38.**G.**
Don. 10/8—14/9/40.**G.**
Don. 4/9—2/10/43.**G.**

BOILERS:
7066.
7092 7/2/20.
7171 *(ex3058)* 13/8/32.
8717 17/3/34.
8534 19/3/38.
D1755 *(exD2 3048)* 14/9/40.
D1751 *(exJ6 3565)* 2/10/43.

SHEDS:
Copley Hill
Grantham ?/?.
Ladybank 18/8/25.
Haymarket 9/25.

Nos.60 and 61 continued to have Ross 'Pop' safety valves although No.60 had a boiler change in January 1920, but the special mounting and safety valves were transferred to the newly built boiler.

Standard buffers on this class were of the parallel shank type with hollow spindle and circular flange, with an overall length of 1ft 6in. There was one change from that type by 1935; No.3064 had a similar NBR type with a collar at the end of the shank. None ever got Group Standard buffers.

A minor change was made to the buffers of four Scottish based engines; Nos.3057, 3058, 3061 and 3064 had thick wooden packing placed between the flange and the beam.

From 1933 some acquired the shorter dome and cover which the Diagram 7 boiler needed when used on the N2 class engines.

On the seven engines returned to the Southern Area, Nos.3052, 3053, 3055, 3056, 3059, 3060 and 3062, Doncaster reduced the cab cut-out to 2ft 5in. and provided a hand grip from 1933. The eight which remained in Scotland did not have any alteration to the cab cut-out.

Boilers built after 1934 were fitted (two each side) with inspection doors and covers instead of washout plugs and the ejector exhaust pipe was placed outside the boiler along the right hand side.

The original and the replacement boilers built up to 1934 had three washout plugs on each side of the firebox. Also the vacuum ejector exhaust pipe was placed within the boiler and not externally.

The standard arrangement of the handrails was along the side of the boiler then curving round the front of the smokebox and then upward, finishing level with a cross rail on the door.

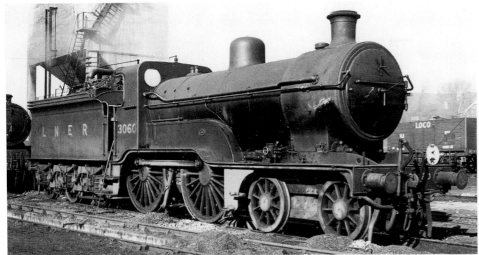

The cross rail position on No.3060 was subject to some fluctuation. This October 1936 photograph shows it below the upper hinge strap, as it was in the photograph on page 10 taken in 1923. However, the previous photograph taken in April 1926 shows it above the strap. Further examples of this non-standard lower position were seen on 3063, 2209 (3058), 2216 (3065).

On one engine, No.62208, Cowlairs replaced the cross rail with the curved type they used for ex-NBR superheated engines. This was maybe due to the fitting of a smokebox number plate in May 1949, the only D1 to get one. The eight which remained in Scotland all kept handrails ending on the smokebox front. Note that 62208 still has Ramsbottom valves.

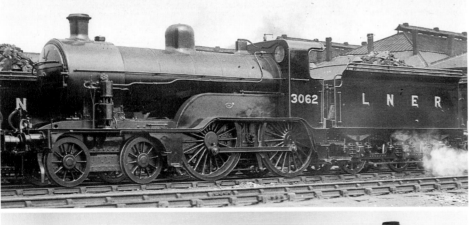

When Doncaster resumed maintenance of the seven returned to Southern Area it started to cut back the handrail on the left hand side to the end on the side of the smokebox. No.3062 was the first to get this modification in July 1933 with the others following, although No.3060 did not get this alteration.

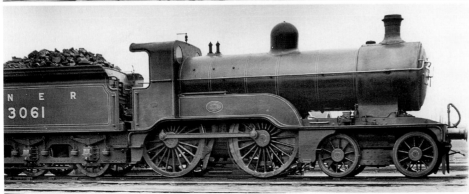

Until 1925 chimneys were 2ft 2¼in. high, of built-up type with the rim 13ft 2⅛in. above rail level. The dome height was 13ft 3⅝in. whilst the whistle was 13ft 1⅝in.

To suit the N.B. gauge and allow the class to be transferred to Scottish Area, a 3in. shorter chimney was fitted, the dome cover got a flatter top, and 2in. was taken out of the whistle stand. This brought the heights down to 12ft 11in., for dome and chimney and 12ft 9⅝in. for the whistle. All were altered and put into LNER livery by Doncaster before re-allocation.

Not until they began working in Scotland was a coach heating connection fitted at the front end. Most had it on the off side of the coupling hook, as on No.3056, but one at least, No.3059 had it on the nearside.

From October 1941 work was found for some of the Southern Area engines on the M&GN and these were equipped with Whittaker tablet exchanging apparatus on the tender.

Standard lubrication was a Wakefield mechanical on the right hand running plate for cylinders and valves. The coupled axleboxes had syphon lubrication. Until 1933 engines stationed at Haymarket and working to Newcastle required to be fitted with Raven fog signalling apparatus. The striker appears to be under the cab, and below the footstep.

3055 continued.
St Margarets 12/28 .
Carlisle 9/31.
Doncaster 9/9/32.
Ipswich 5/10/33.
Norwich 3/7/36.
Yarmouth Beach 25/10/41.

RENUMBERED:
  55N 29/9/23.
  3055 25/7/25.
  2206 allocated.

CONDEMNED: 15/6/46.
Cut up at Doncaster.

3056

Doncaster 1301.

To traffic 4/1911.

REPAIRS:
Don. 3/8—19/11/21.**G.**
Don. 21/2—9/8/24.**G.**
Don. 3/11/24—12/3/25.**L.**
Cow. ?/?—3/27.**L.**
Westinghouse fitted.
Cowlairs data missing.
Cow. 9/3—4/4/31.**G.**
Don. 15/7—19/8/33.**G.**
Don. 13/7—3/8/35.**G.**
Don. 13/3—10/4/37.**G.**
West. to vacuum brake.
Don. 1/4—6/5/39.**G.**
Don. 25/9—16/10/43.**G.**
Don. 17/3—7/4/45.**L.**
Don. 23/3—13/4/46.**G.**

BOILERS:
  7067.
  7074 *(ex3063)* 9/8/24.
D1761 *(exJ6 3636)* 19/8/33.
  7675 6/5/39.
  9612 13/4/46.

SHEDS:
Cambridge
Doncaster 5/10/24.
Carlisle 27/3/25.
Doncaster 23/4/31.
Ipswich 11/10/33.
Norwich 17/7/36.
Cambridge 26/5/40.
Norwich 15/5/41.
Melton Constable 25/10/41.
Norwich 29/10/41.
Melton Constable 5/12/41.
Norwich 28/3/42.
Yarmouth Beach 19/8/45.
Norwich 22/9/45.
Melton Constable 18/7/46.
Norwich 31/7/46.
Melton Constable 11/8/46.
Norwich 22/9/46.

Yarmouth Beach 27/9/46.
Norwich 23/6/48.

RENUMBERED:
3056 9/8/24.
2207 5/1/47.

CONDEMNED: 8/11/48
Cut up at Doncaster.

3057

Doncaster 1302.

To traffic 5/1911.

REPAIRS:
Don. 25/9/22—6/1/23.**G.**
Don. 21/2—24/3/23.**L.**
Don. 8/12/24—20/2/25.**G.**
Cow. ?/?—1/3/26.**L.**
Westinghouse fitted.
Cow. ?/8—?/10/27.**G.**
Cowlairs data missing.
Cow. ?/?—7/31.**L.**
Cow. 23/9—1/11/33.**G.**
Cow. 2/41-8/3/41.**G.**
Westinghouse to steam brake.
Cow. 27/11/43—22/1/44.**G.**
Cow. 26/4—16/5/47.**L.**
Cow. 24—31/1/48.**C/H.**
Cow. 12—17/4/48.**L.**
Cow. 31/3—20/5/49.**L/I.**

BOILERS:
7068.
7063 *(ex3052)* 20/2/25.
8692 *as C1534* 1/11/33.
9136 *(new)* 8/3/41.
8279 *(ex3065)* 22/1/44.
7064 *(ex2212)* 31/1/48.

SHEDS:
Grantham
St Margarets 23/2/25.
Thornton Jct. 5/3/25.
Carlisle *by* 12/26.
Haymarket ?/4/34.
Hawick *by* 3/36.

RENUMBERED
  3057 20/2/25.
  2208 22/12/46.
  62208 17/4/48.

CONDEMNED: 13/7/50.

3058

Doncaster 1303.

To traffic 5/1911.

REPAIRS:
Don. 2/7—22/10/21.**G.**

Don. 20/7—17/11/23.**G.**
Don. 27/4—25/7/25.**G.**
Cow. ?/12/26—?/3/27.**G.**
Westinghouse fitted.
Cow. ?/?—5/10/29.**G.**
Cow. ?/9/31—?/10/31.**G.**
Cow. 28/10/33—?/?/??.**?.**
Cow. ?/?—3/7/36.**G.**
Cow. ?/?—22/8/38.**G.**
Cow. 8/2—8/3/41.**G.**
Cow. 11/7—21/8/45.**G.**
Westinghouse to steam brake.
Not in use 318 days in 1944 and
145 in 1945. Stored 2/1-17/7/49.

BOILERS:
7069.
7062 *(ex3051)* 17/11/23.
7070 *(ex3059)* ?/3/27.
7171 *(ex3051)* 5/10/29.
7091 *(ex3051)* ?/10/31.
7062 *(ex3054)* 8/3/41.
8810 *(ex3051)* 21/8/45.

SHEDS:
Grantham
Carlisle 19/8/25.
Thornton Jct. *by* 12/25.
Carlisle 30/6/28.
Haymarket 13/6/45.
Stirling 29/6/46.

RENUMBERED
  58N 17/11/23.
  3058 25/7/25.
  2209 9/6/46.

CONDEMNED: 11/11/50.

3059

Doncaster 1304.

To traffic 5/1911.

REPAIRS:
Don. 3/11/21—25/3/22.**G.**
Don. 3/3/23.**L.**
Don. 30/10/23—23/2/24.**G.**
Cow. ?/?—?/10/25.**G.**
Cow. ?/?—?/1/26.**N/C.**
Westinghouse fitted.
Cowlairs data missing.
Cow. 4—28/2/31.**G.**
Don. 5—23/5/31.**L.**
Don. 12/8—7/10/33.**G.**
Don. 28/3—25/4/36.**G.**
Don. 17/4—29/5/37.**L.**
Engine brake reverted to
vacuum.
Don. 30/7—27/8/38.**G.**
Don. 20/6—18/7/42.**G.**
Don. 10/4—1/5/43.**L.**
Don. 19/5—16/6/45.**G.**

BOILERS:
7070.
7395 10/25.
8941 25/4/36.
8567 *(exD2 4399)* 16/6/45.

SHEDS:
Grantham
Eastfield 22/1/25.
Thorton Jct. 19/3/25.
Carlisle *by* 12/26.
Doncaster 13/3/31.
Norwich 10/6/31.
Peterborough East 26/5/32.
New England 23/11/32.
Boston 14/4/33.
Norwich 24/10/33.
Cambridge 26/5/40.
Norwich 1/4/41.
Yarmouth Beach 15/6/47.

RENUMBERED:
3059 23/2/24.
2210 5/1/47.

CONDEMNED: 23/12/47.
Cut up at Doncaster.

3060

Doncaster 1305.

To traffic 5/1911.

REPAIRS:
Don. ?/?—1/20.**G.**
Don. 9/11/22—3/2/23.**G.**
Don. 12—27/10/23.**L.**
Don. 24/2—13/6/25.**G.**
Cow. ?/?—?/12/27.**G.**
Westinghouse fitted.
Cow. 14/10—?/12/28.**L.**
Cow. ?/?—17/8/29.**G.**
Cow. ?/?—16/9/32.**G.**
Don. 26/5—30/6/34.**G.**
Raven F.S.A. removed.
Don. 23/1—13/2/37.**G.**
West. to vacuum brake.
Don. 19/3—16/4/38.**G.**
Don. 25/7—15/8/42.**G.**
Don. 13/1—24/3/45.**G.**

BOILERS:
7071.
7417 ?/1/20.
8565 16/9/32.
8710 16/4/38.
8271 15/8/42.
9062 24/3/45.

SHEDS:
Cambridge
Haymarket 22/6/25.
Dundee *by* 20/4/29.
Doncaster 20/9/32.

Replacement boilers built after 1931 used only Ross 'Pop' safety valves and with these on Nos.3051, 3054, 3057, 3059 and 3062, Cowlairs provided their own circular cover around the base. They looked wrong and were not needed as the 'Pops' were mounted directly on to the firebox casing. Eventually the five engines which got them were to lose them.

In line with GNR practice, twin lamp irons were provided at the right hand front end when built. Note No.3062 got to Perth shed without having its whistle height altered.

Only Nos.3057 and 3058 had lost the redundant lamp iron by the time the class went to Scotland but once there, they were gradually removed. One, however, No.2205 kept the redundant iron to its 1948 withdrawal. Note that the GN load class W is still being shown in the 1930s by the collar on the vacuum standpipe.

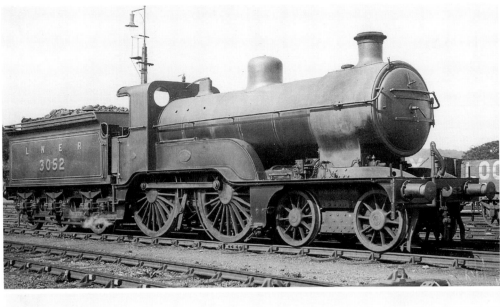

(left) One of No.3052's first duties in Scotland was banking trains from Inverkeithing up to the Forth Bridge. This required a slip coupling, and a bracket for the operating wire was put on the smokebox by its shed at Dunfermline.

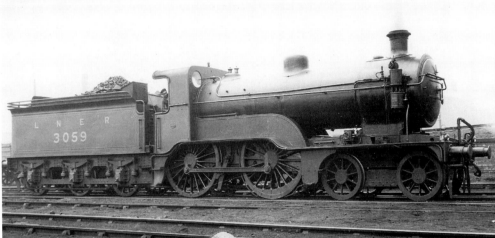

(centre) Originally, and for a full year after their transfer to Scotland began, the brake was vacuum only, for both engine and train. Beginning with No.3062 (31/10/25), 3059 (1/26) and 3057 (1/3/26), the brake was altered and a Westinghouse pump was put on, with vacuum retained for alternative train braking. These three had the pump placed high on the right side of the smokebox, and a platform step was put on the running plate to help access for oiling the pump.

(below) This pump position was found to interfere with the driver's forward vision, so on the next installations the pump was moved to the left side but still in a high position and with platform step on the running plate.

3060 continued.
Boston 29/7/33.
Ipswich 27/8/35.
Norwich 6/7/36.
Cambridge 26/5/40 .
Norwich 1/4/41.
Melton Constable 24/10/41.
Norwich 4/11/41.
Yarmouth Beach 27/5/45.
Norwich 11/8/45.

RENUMBERED:
60N 27/10/23.
3060 3/2/25.
2211 allocated.

CONDEMNED: 11/12/46.
Cut up at Doncaster.

3061

Doncaster 1306.

To traffic 5/1911.

REPAIRS:
Don. 11/11/20—2/4/21.**G**.
Don. 22/2—26/7/24.**G**.
Don. 15/1—7/2/25.**L**.
Cow. ?/?—29/10/27.**G**.
Westinghouse fitted.
Cowlairs data missing.
Cow. ?/?—29/12/34.**H**.
Cow. ?/?—1/12/36.**G**.
Cow. ?/?—?/9/39.**G**.
Cow. 21/10/39.**N/C**.
A.R.P. screens fitted.
Cow. 25/7—5/9/42.**G**.
Not in use all 1944 and 163 days in 1945.Stored 15/2/46.

BOILERS:
7072.
7400 *(exDon)* 29/10/27.
9133 *(new)* 9/39.
7064 *(ex3064)* 5/9/42.

SHEDS:
Cambridge
Eastfield 10/2/25.
Haymarket *by* 18/9/25.
Carlisle 12/33.
Haymarket 13/6/45.

RENUMBERED:
3061 26/7/24.
2212 27/4/46.

CONDEMNED: 5/7/47.

3062

Doncaster 1307.

To traffic 6/1911.

REPAIRS:
Don. 18/4—13/5/22.**L**.
Don. 22/2—30/6/23.**G**.
Don. 22/6—8/8/25.**G**.
Don. 19—31/10/25.**L**.
Westinghouse fitted.
Cow. ?/?—31/12/28.**G**.
Cow. 6/6—10/7/31.**G**.
Don. 3/6—1/7/33.**H**.
Don. 18/4—9/5/36.**G**.
Don. 3—10/4/37.**L**.
West. to vacuum brake.
Don. 26/11—17/12/38.**G**.
Don. 8/7—22/7/39.**H**.
Don. 27/12/41—7/2/42.**G**.
Don. 10/4—26/6/43.**G**.
Don. 1/6/46. *Not repaired.*

BOILERS:
7073.
7091 30/6/23.
7072 *(ex3061)* 31/12/28.
D1782 *(exJ6 3544)* 1/7/33.
D1780 *(exJ6 3625)* 9/5/36.
8546 22/7/39.

SHEDS:
Grantham
Cambridge 17/5/22.
To Scotland 3/10/25.
Perth 30/10/25.
Doncaster 14/7/31.
Norwich 7/8/31.
Peterborough East 19/5/32.
New England 13/12/32.
Peterborough East 7/7/33.
Boston 4/10/33.
Peterborough East 16/4/35.
Ipswich 28/8/35.
Norwich 9/7/36.
Cambridge 26/5/40.
Norwich 1/4/41.
Melton Constable 28/3/42.
Yarmouth Beach 11/2/45.

RENUMBERED:
3062 8/8/25.
2213 allocated.

CONDEMNED: 18/6/46.
Cut up at Doncaster.

3063

Doncaster 1308

To traffic 6/1911

REPAIRS:
Don. 13/5—31/7/20.**G**.
Don. 20/4—28/7/23.**G**.
Don. 16/4—18/7/25.**G**.
Cow. ?/?—9/27.**L**.
Westinghouse fitted.
Cow. ?/?—9/28.**G**.

Cow. ?/?—8/31.**G**.
Cow. ?/?—3/11/34.**G**.
Cow. ?/?—25/12/37.**G**.
Cow. ?/?—31/8/39.**G**.
Cow. ?/?—15/11/41.**H**.
Cow. 3—21/7/45.**G**.
Converted from Westinghouse to steam brake.
Not in use for 318 days in 1944 & 149 days in 1945.
Stored in tallow 6/2—7/8/49.

BOILERS:
7074.
7179 28/7/23.
7073 *(ex3065)* ?/9/28.
7177 *(ex3054)* 3/11/34.
7063 *(ex3065)* 31/8/39.
9136 *(ex3057)* 21/7/45.

SHEDS:
New England.
Haymarket 24/7/25.
Hawick 8/37.
Carlisle 13/3/40.
Haymarket 13/6/45.
Stirling 4/46.
Haymarket 26/6/46.
Hawick 27/9/48.

RENUMBERED:
3063 18/7/25.
2214 30/6/46.

CONDEMNED: 16/9/49.
Into Cowlairs for c/u 6/10/49.

3064

Doncaster 1309

To traffic 6/1911

REPAIRS:
Don. 13/11/22—17/2/23.**G**.
Don. 13/3—20/6/25.**G**.
Cow. 11/2—12/3/27.**G**.
Westinghouse fitted.
Cow. ?/?—3/10/31.**G**.
Cowlairs data missing.
Cow. 13/2—20/3/37.**H**.
Fog apparatus removed.
Cow. 21/2—21/3/42.**H**.
Cow. ?/?—13/11/43.**H**.
Converted from Westinghouse to steam brake.
Cow. 27/6—16/7/45.**H**.
Cow. 8/12/45—11/1/46.**G**.
Cow. 20/6—18/7/47.**H**.
Cow. 12/3—20/8/48.**L**.
Stored in tallow 16/5—18/9/49.

BOILERS:
7075.
7067 *(ex3056)* 20/6/25.

7064 *(ex3054)* 3/10/31.
C1534 *(ex3057)* 21/3/42.
7062 *(ex3058)* 11/1/46.

SHEDS:
New England.
Haymarket 20/6/25.
Hawick 28/11/42.
Perth 12/43.
Perth (LMS) 18/9/49.
Perth (LNE) 24/1/50.

RENUMBERED:
3064 20/6/25.
2215 13/10/46.
62215 20/3/48.

CONDEMNED: 10/2/50.

3065

Doncaster 1310

To traffic 7/1911

REPAIRS:
Don. 25/10/22—3/2/23.**G**.
Don. 3/3—26/6/25.**G**.
Cow. ?/?—4/27.**G**.
Westinghouse fitted.
Cowlairs data incomplete.
Cow. ?/?—4/11/33.**G**.
Cow. ?/?—18/12/37.**H**.
Cow. 4/6—16/6/38.**G**.
Cow. ?/?—15/8/39.**L**.
Cow. ?/?—5/4/40.**L**.
Cow. ?/?—10/8/40.**L**.
Cow. ?/?—26/12/42.**G**.
Converted from Westinghouse to steam brake.
Stored 28/9/46 to await decision.

BOILERS:
7076.
7073 *(ex??)* 26/6/25.
7062 *(ex3058)* ?/4/27.
7063 *(ex3057)* 4/11/33.
8279 *(exD2 4382)* 16/6/38.
8534 *(ex3055)* 26/12/42

SHEDS:
New England.
Haymarket 26/6/25.
Hawick 30/11/36.
Haymarket 5/38.
Polmont 1/42.
Hawick 5/42.

RENUMBERED:
3065 31/1/25.
2216 17/11/46

CONDEMNED: 5/9/47.

These later installations divided into two groups, No.3051 being ex Cowlairs 16th July and No.3052 on 28th August 1926. Note that their platform step differed in detail, 3051 having a crossbar.

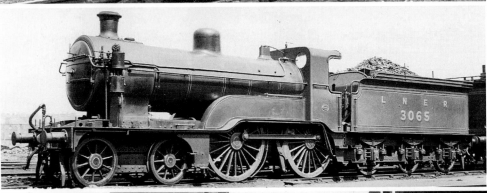

No more had a pump put on for six months but in 1927 another group of four got the brake change with the pump in the same position and with a platform step provided. They were 3064 and 3058 (both March), and 3054 and 3065 (both April). As No.3056 was also Westinghouse fitted in March 1927, it seems probable it would be the same as the four which have been checked.

The other five to complete the brake change in 1927 were Nos.3053 (August), 3055 (July), 3063 (September), 3061 (October) and 3060 (December). All had the pump placed low down which then became the standard position and the earlier fitted engines all changed to it as and when convenient.

When No.3064's pump position was changed in June 1929 the consequent gap in the handrail was not then given any attention but when next ex works on 3rd October 1931 it had been tidied up. Those engines which returned to Southern Area had their Westinghouse equipment removed beginning in February 1937 and they reverted to vacuum brakes for engine and train.

Six of the eight engines in Scottish Area also had a late change to their brakes, only Nos.3051 and 3061 retaining Westinghouse to withdrawal. The others went to steam brake for the engine but kept vacuum for train brakes. They were Nos.3054 (1/44), 3057 (3/41), 3058 (8/45), 3063 (7/45), 3064 (11/43) and 3065 (12/42).

When the class went to Scotalnd in 1925/6, the tenders with Nos.3060 and 3065 were Class B 3670 gallon type with equally spaced axles, which had been built in 1901.

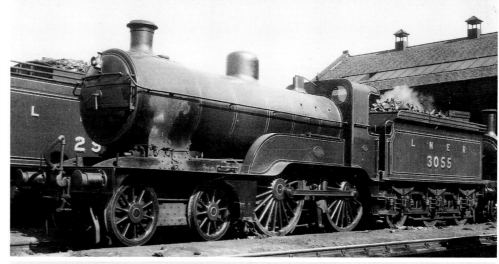

Seven, Nos.3051, 3054, 3055, 3056, 3057, 3058 and 3059 took with them Class A 3000 gallon tenders which had equal 6ft 6in. axle spacings. Note that the plating behind the coalrail extends to the front curve, and Nos.3051, 3056 and 3059 also had this type.

On the other tenders of this type, the plating stopped at the end of the coal space, not quite meeting the slope of the front plate. Nos.3054, 3057 and 3058 were those with this variation.

The other six, Nos.3052, 3053, 3061, 3062, 3063 and 3064, took the later Class A tender which was also a 3000 gallon type but which had 6ft 10½in. and 6ft 1½in. spacing for the axles.

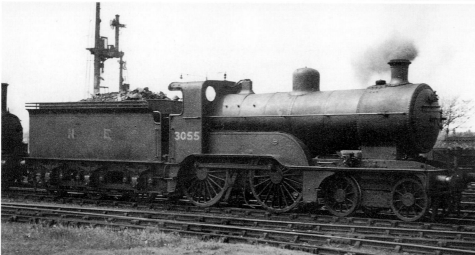

Both Cowlairs and Doncaster subsequently made tender changes. From 2nd October 1943 No.3055 had a later Class A tender with unequal axle spacing.

(below) At Grouping the whole class were in GNR fully lined green passenger livery.

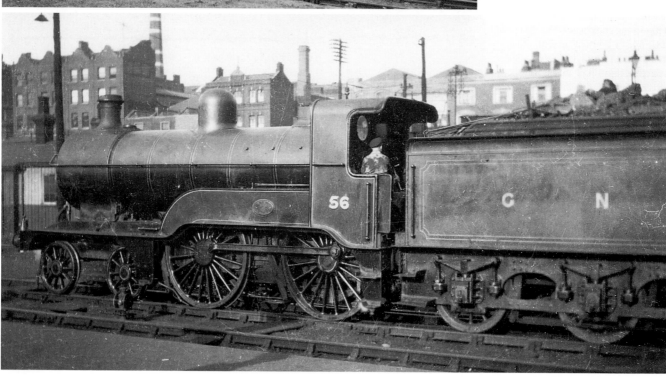

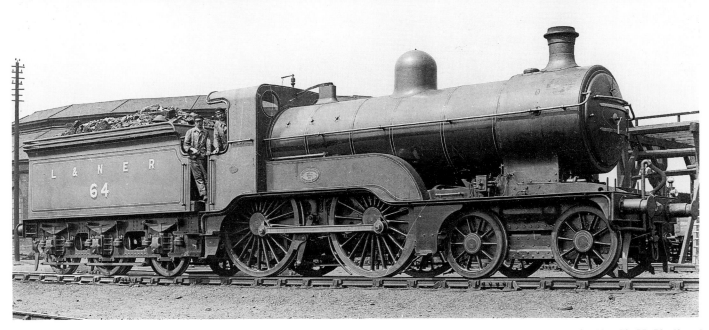

No.64 in the L&NER fully lined green livery. Nos.60 and 65 were in similar style, but the ampersand was dropped for Nos.53, 55, 58, 62 and 63. Note the tender lining of No.64 has rounded corners compared with the GN scalloped corners. Also note the different tenders, No.56 in the previous photograph has no cut out in the top corner of the cab end whilst No.64 has the cut out and the lining has been altered accordingly. Only three D1's had the N suffix added to their numbers - 55 (29/9/23), 58 (17/11/23) and 60 (27/10/23). No.60 received an N at a light repair, so it was exceptional in being in combination with L&NER on the tender. The other seven went direct to LNER and 1924 numbers with 3000 added:- 3051 (5/2/25), 3052 (25/9/24), 3054 (23/8/24), 3056 (9/8/24), 3057 (20/2/25), 3059 (23/2/24) and 3061 (26/7/24).

By the time of the transfer to Scotland, all had LNER green livery and their new number. However with the painting economies of 1928 coming into force the first D1 to lose its lined green livery was No.3063 in September 1928 when it was turned out in unlined black with number still on the tender. Others with this style applied were 3052, 3055, 3056, 3057, 3060 and 3062. In the meantime No.3061 still had its fully lined green livery when seen 23rd March 1933: it was not ex works again until 29th December 1934.

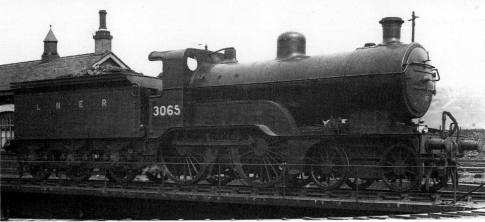

In May 1930 No.3065 which got its cab number in July 1929, was paired with the tender from No.3055 which had been painted black in December 1928. The 3055 number on the tender was blacked out but LNER in the high position was left undisturbed.

21

From May 1929, starting that month with No.3051, the number was moved from tender to cab and at first Cowlairs used 10in. shaded figures. On the tender they continued to use the 7½in. shaded LNER.

(*left*) When No.3055 was ex Cowlairs on 13th August 1932 they managed to put 12in. numbers on the cab and with very few exceptions thereafter they used 12in. through to their final D1 numbering in May 1949 (*see* 62208 on page 12).

(*below*) Only a month after No.3055 got 12in. numbers it left Scotland and became Doncaster maintained, but that works persisted using 9in. figures on D1 cabs and applied 12in. letters to the tenders.

The red lining used in conjunction with black paint ceased to be used from November 1941 and between June 1942 and January 1946 only NE was put on the tenders. Doncaster made no change to the size of either numbers or letters. No.3060 was ex works 24th March 1945.

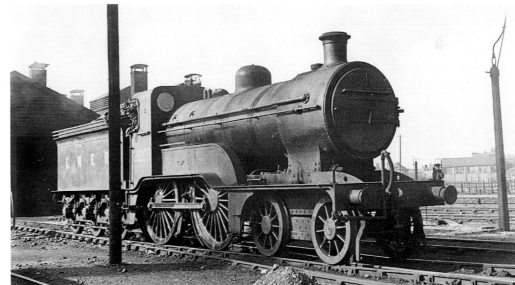

No.2207 (ex3056) was not renumbered until Sunday 5th January 1947 but had regained LNER when ex works on 13th April 1946. The use of 12in. shaded transfers was probably due to very late renumbering date. This also applied to 2203 and 2210, the only others in the Southern Area which got 1946 numbers.

Although all the Scottish re-numberings were done at the sheds, 12in. shaded transfers were found for them. However, most of their tenders had not been repainted after 1941, and (where it could be discerned) continued to carry 7½in. LNER through to withdrawal.

Despite the lamentable state into which the "painting" was allowed to deteriorate, the information on their buffer beam continued to be presented properly. Their new numbers were put on in 4½in. shaded transfers and after the word 'class' was dropped in 1943, the shed name was added, in 1½in. white lettering.

The last of the class to be withdrawn - on 11th November 1950 - still had 7½in. LNER on its tender and never got any BR renumbering. However, it did get a BR cast shed allocation plate fitted to its smokebox door. This was 63B Stirling.

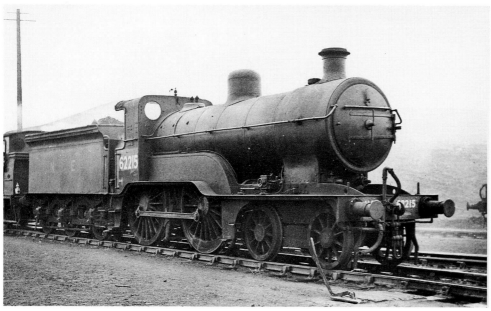

Alone amongst the Scottish engines to deviate from the 7½in. tender lettering were No.3064 which got 12in. NE when ex Cowlairs 11th January 1946 and No.2208 which on 31st January 1948 came out with 12in. LNER (*see* photo on page 12). Both duly acquired full BR number, 62215 on 20th March 1948 and 62208 on 17th April 1948, in unshaded Gill sans but with modified 6.

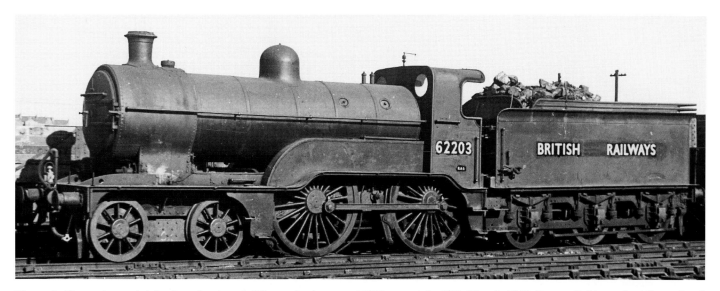

The only Doncaster maintained engine to get BR numbering was 62203, ex works 25th March 1948, from a light repair. 10in. painted unshaded characters were used including modified 6. As it survived until 31st August 1950 it duly acquired a cast shed plate.

From 5th January 1942 No.3053 worked out of Melton Constable shed but at an unrecorded date moved to Yarmouth Beach shed, probably in January 1945. From there it was withdrawn on 9th March 1946 and it arrived at Doncaster for scrapping on 22nd March. When this photograph was taken at the works on 22nd June, scrapping had not proceeded very far. the boiler was however used on N2 class 9576, ex works 11th April 1947 and the tender had gone to D2 No.4366. No.3053 was to be 2204 but never carried that number.

Ex Doncaster 25th March 1948 as 62203, it was the only one to get BRITISH RAILWAYS on the tender. On 6th November 1949 it left Melton Constable and moved to Colwick and worked Nottingham to Grantham stopping trains. Withdrawn on 31st August 1950, 62203 was the only one of the fifteen to finish its career at a former GNR shed. It went to Doncaster for scrapping but on 22nd October 1950 they passed it on to Darlington and here on that day it had just entered their scrap yard. Disposal was not however completed until 10th February 1951.

A further ten engines Nos.1326 to 1335 were also built in 1898. Tender shows paint date as 19-11-98. Note flat coupling rod, and curved running plate without the extra casing, all following engines being built this way.

(left) Ten engines Nos.1336 to 1340 and 1361 to 1365 were built in 1899 and were the same as the previous batch. Note destination board brackets fitted above the cross rail on the smokebox door for use in the Nottingham area.

(below) Twenty further engines Nos.1366 to 1385 were built during the period from October to December 1900 and these were also the same as previous batches. Note that no door was provided between the cab and tender and the latter is the new 3670 gallon Class B.

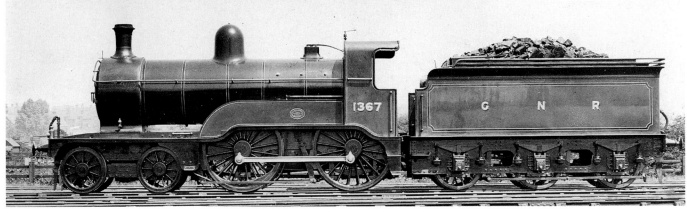

CLASS D 2

4305

Rebuilt from D3 at Doncaster.

To traffic 29/10/23.

REPAIRS:
Don. 26/10/25—16/1/26.**G.**
Don. 14/2—25/6/28.**G.**
Don. 17/5—18/7/30.**G.**
Cab sides altered.
Don. 1/10—29/11/32.**G.**
Don. 11/5—29/6/35.**G.**
Don. 26/4—27/5/38.**G.**
Don. 21/3—24/4/40.**G.**
Don. 20/1—22/2/41.**L.**
After collision.
Don. 23/4—16/5/42.**G.**
Don. 26/2—1/4/44.**G.**
Don. 2/11—1/12/45.**G.**
Don. 20/6—15/8/47.**G.**

BOILERS:
6978.
7401 25/6/28.
8394 29/6/35.
8414 27/5/38.
9203 24/4/40.
8879 1/4/44.
9002 1/12/45.

SHEDS:
Colwick.
Leicester 24/10/35.
Colwick 15/3/38.
Langwith Jct 13/7/40.
Colwick 13/11/40.

RENUMBERED:
1305N 29/10/23.
4305 16/1/26.
2150 10/11/46.

CONDEMNED: 23/5/49.

4320

Rebuilt from D3 at Doncaster.

To traffic 15/7/26

REPAIRS:
Don. 11/10—7/12/28.**G.**
Don. 19/2—11/5/31.**G.**
Cab sides altered.
Don. 3/7—23/9/33.**G.**
Front heater connection fitted.
Don. 21/12/35—25/1/36.**G.**
Don. 10/3—14/4/38.**G.**
Don. 9/5—9/6/40.**G.**
Don. 22/7—3/8/42.**G.**

Don. 22/12/44—8/2/45.**G.**
Don. 21/10/46—5/9/47.**G.**
Don. 28/4/49. *Not repaired.*

BOILERS:
7169.
7109 11/5/31.
8002 23/9/33.
7753 14/4/38.
8388 9/6/40.
8706 3/8/42.
8419 8/2/45.

SHEDS:
Colwick.
Hitchin 22/8/33.
Retford 15/3/34.
Boston 9/5/34.
Lincoln 5/11/34.
Louth 2/2/37.
Colwick 12/6/37.
Leicester 23/7/37.
Colwick 27/8/37.
Langwith Jct 13/11/40.
Colwick 17/9/41.

RENUMBERED:
4320 *whilst Class D3.*
2151 27/10/46.

CONDEMNED: 30/4/49.
Cut up at Doncaster.

4321

Doncaster 770.

To traffic 6/1898.

REPAIRS:
Don. ?/?—2/03.**G.**
Don. ?/?—10/07.**G.**
Don. ?/?—6/19.**G.**
Don. 12/10/21—14/1/22.**G.**
Don. 5/4—16/6/23.**L.**
Don. 23/2—16/5/25.**G.**
Don. 2/11—12/12/28.**G.**
Don. 17/10—14/11/31.**G.**
Cab sides altered.
Don. 18/8—8/9/34.**G.**
Don. 8—15/1/38.**G.**
Don. 22/5—19/6/43.**G.**
Don. 15—29/1/44.**L.**
Don. 21/8—3/10/47.**G.**
Don. 5/1/49. *Not repaired.*

BOILERS:
1321.
1492 2/03.
1327 10/07.
7407 6/19.

7396 12/12/28.
8387 15/1/38.
8392 3/10/47.

SHEDS:
King's Cross.
New England 24/12/28.
Retford 17/3/32.
King's Cross 1/9/34.
Hitchin 12/9/34.
New England 4/1/35.
Boston 24/11/36.
New England 17/12/36.
Peterborough East 24/12/36.
New England 6/1/37.
South Lynn 10/1/37.
New England 2/3/37.
South Lynn 10/7/37.
March 27/11/37.
South Lynn 21/6/38.
March 28/9/38.
South Lynn 23/5/39.
King's Lynn 19/10/39.
South Lynn 9/6/40.
March 9/2/41.
South Lynn 20/5/42.
Yarmouth 4/3/45.
Norwich 29/4/45.
Melton Constable 27/5/45.
Norwich 19/8/45.
Yarmouth Beach 27/8/45.

RENUMBERED
4321 16/5/25.
2152 24/10/46

CONDEMNED: 8/1/49.
Cut up at Doncaster.

4322

Doncaster 771.

To traffic 6/1898.

REPAIRS:
Don. ?/?—12/03.**G.**
Don. ?/?—12/09.**G.**
Don. ?/?—3/18.**G.**
Don. 10/11/21—11/2/22.**G.**
Don. 10/10/24—10/1/25.**G.**
Don. 25/7—11/10/27.**G.**
Don. 22/6—27/7/29.**G.**
Cab sides altered.
Don. 13/6—18/7/31.**G.**
Don. 1/4—13/5/33.**G.**
Don. 12—26/1/35.**G.**
Don. 6/3—3/4/37.**G.**
Don. 24/6/39. *Not repaired.*

BOILERS:
1322.
1495 12/03.
1416 12/09.
6870 3/18.
8002 11/10/27.
8701 13/5/33.
8418 3/4/37.

SHEDS:
King's Cross (Hitchin).
Retford 28/10/27.
Colwick 26/1/35.
New England 2/4/37.
New England (MGN) 23/4/37.
New England 7/5/37.
South Lynn 13/5/37.

RENUMBERED:
4322 10/1/25.

CONDEMNED: 4/7/39.
Cut up at Doncaster.

4323

Doncaster 772.

To traffic 6/1898.

REPAIRS:
Don. ?/?—10/03.**G.**
Don. ?/?—11/09.**G.**
Don. 20/11/19—10/4/20.**G.**
Don. 2/11/23—19/1/24.**G.**
Don. 15/6—5/9/25.**L.**
Don. 12/2—4/5/27.**G.**
Don. 24/11/28—26/1/29.**G.**
Don. 13/9—8/11/30.**G.**
Cab sides altered.
Don. 7/12/32—25/2/33.**G.**
Don. 16/11—22/12/34.**G.**
Don. 2/2—12/3/38.**G.**
Don. 28/11—28/12/40.**G.**
Don. 6/3—8/4/44.**G.**
Don. 30/11/45—26/1/46.**G.**
Don. 5/8—3/9/46.**H.**

BOILERS:
1323.
1321 10/03.
1413 11/09.
7006 10/4/20.
7993 4/5/27.
7753 25/2/33.
8190 12/3/38.
8390 8/4/44.
8415 26/1/46.

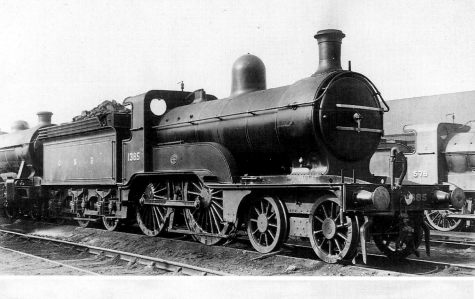

(above) **It seems probable that No.1369 was the first one to be fitted with a door between the cab and tender, a provision which became a standard safety feature. The tender is a 3170 gallon Class A type.**

No.1385, the last engine of the 1900 batch seen as running at Grouping and coupled with a Stirling design tender which had three coal rails and wooden buffer beam. Note upper lamp iron on top of smokebox and twin irons at the front right hand corner for use in the London district.

Ten more engines Nos.1386 to 1395 were built January to June 1903 followed in August and September 1907 by five more, Nos.1396 to 1399 and 1180, to the same basic design but had parallel shank buffers.

A final batch of ten, Nos.41 to 50 were built March to May 1909 to same design as the 1907 build. No tenders were built specifically for these and this one is a Stirling Class C with three coal rails and wooden buffer beam.

No.4305 originally of D3 class but rebuilt and added to D2 class as No.1305ₙ in October 1923. Note that it retained straight running plate and casing for coupling rod.

As spare frames were available, one more D3 No.4320 was rebuilt to D2 in June 1926.

The first five engines Nos.4321 to 4325 kept the straight running plate to withdrawal, three of them even to 1949/50. The first of the rebuilds from D3, No.4305 also retained its straight running plate to its May 1949 withdrawal as No.2150. All the others including the other rebuild, No.4320, kept the curved running plate without alteration to it.

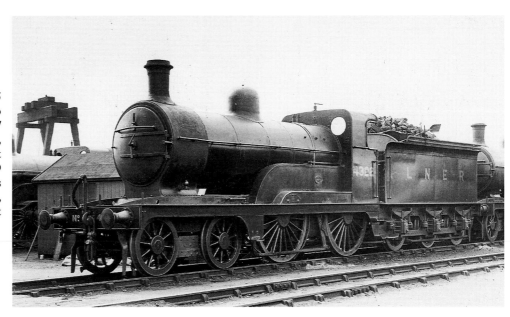

Those with a curved running plate through to No.4395 had a footstep provided on the front of the leading curve. The last fifteen engines Nos.4396 to 4399 and 3041 to 3050 were not so fitted and never had the footstep put on.

In April 1914 No.1381 was fitted with a Robinson superheater, Gresley anti-vacuum valve, balanced slide valves, and a Wakefield mechanical lubricator.

Shortage of replacement boilers led to three of the class being superheated in 1928, No.4378 (February) and 4334 with 4399 in May. They kept flat valves but were fitted with mechanical lubricator. Steam for the anti-carboniser was taken from the blower valve on the side of the smokebox. Nos. 4378 and 4399 got the Wakefield type lubricator whilst the third engine No.4334 got the Hulburb mechanical lubricator. All three had Ramsbottom safety valves although the boilers were new and two had been built at Darlington.

4323 continued.
SHEDS:
York.
Ardsley 12/23.
New England 14/1/26.
Grantham *by* 1/31.
Louth 28/6/39.
Colwick 29/8/43.
Staveley 24/3/46.
Colwick 28/9/47.

RENUMBERED:
1323N 19/1/24.
4323 5/9/25.
2153 22/9/46.

CONDEMNED: 9/4/49.

4324

Doncaster 773.

To traffic 6/1898.

REPAIRS:
Don. ?/?—7/04.**G.**
Don. ?/?—1/18.**G.**
Don. 22/4—13/8/21.**G.**
Don. 27/6—17/10/24.**G.**
Don. 29/4—26/8/26.**G.**
Don. 1/7/28—5/2/29.**G.**
Don. 21/12/29—15/2/30.**G.**
Cab sides altered.
Don. 23/3—30/7/32.**G.**
Don. 23/8—24/9/32.**L.**
Don. 28/8—12/10/35.**G.**
Don. 6—29/1/38.**G.**
Don. 23/9—22/10/38.**L.**
Don. 2—30/11/40.**G.**
Don. 15/12/43—22/1/44.**G.**
Don. 31/8—17/10/47.**G.**

BOILERS:
1324.
1598 7/04.
1373 1/18.
6977 13/8/21.
7419 5/2/29.
8534 30/7/32.
8000 29/1/38.
8414 30/11/40.
8331 17/10/47.

SHEDS:
Retford.
New England 30/5/32.
Boston 23/10/33.
Grantham 5/4/34.
Boston 12/6/39.

RENUMBERED:
4324 17/10/24.
2154 15/12/46

CONDEMNED: 22/11/50.

4325

Doncaster 774.

To traffic 7/1898.

REPAIRS:
Don. ?/?—11/03.**G.**
Don. ?/?—4/07.**G.**
Don. ?/?—11/10.**G.**
Don. ?/?—6/18.**G.**
Don. 21/7—16/10/20.**G.**
Don. 12/8—31/10/25.**G.**
Don. 12/1—23/2/29.**G.**
Don. 23/7—20/8/32.**G.**
Cab sides altered.
Don. 24/11—15/12/34.**G.**

BOILERS:
1325.
1494 11/03.
1333 4/07.
1381 11/10.
1598 6/18.
8188 23/2/29.

SHEDS:
Doncaster.
Lincoln ?/?
Immingham 21/1/27.
Louth 23/7/27.
Lincoln 17/11/37.

RENUMBERED:
4325 31/10/25.

CONDEMNED: 10/12/37.

4326

Doncaster 785.

To traffic 10/1898.

REPAIRS:
Don. ?/?—6/04.**G.**
Don. ?/?—1/16.**G.**
Don. 9/3—8/7/22.**G.**
Don. 16/11/25—20/2/26.**G.**
Don. 12/5—25/7/28.**G.**
Don. 2/8—30/8/30.**G.**
Cab sides altered.
Don. 2/6—30/6/34.**G.**
Don. 12/12—31/12/36.**G.**
Don. 5/10—2/11/40.**G.**
Don. 22/5—26/6/43.**G.**
Don. 15/12/45—12/1/46.**G.**
Don. 6/7—20/7/46.**L.**

BOILERS:
1326.
1599 6/04.
1414 1/16.
7211 20/2/26.
7249 25/7/28.

7756 30/6/34.
8708 2/11/40.
8884 26/6/43.

SHEDS:
Copley Hill.
Hitchin 6/1/24.
Colwick 26/2/35.
New England 29/12/36.
New England (MGN) 12/1/37.
Melton Constable 20/1/37.
Norwich 20/11/37.
Melton Constable 30/4/38.
Norwich 10/10/38.
Melton Constable 9/6/39.
Yarmouth Beach 8/2/41.
Melton Constable 4/5/41.
Norwich 11/4/42.
Melton Constable 29/4/42.

RENUMBERED:
4326 20/2/26.
2155 28/9/46

CONDEMNED: 26/2/48.

4327

Doncaster 786.

To traffic 10/1898.

REPAIRS:
Don. ?/?—1/05.**G.**
Don. ?/?—11/11.**G.**
Don. ?/?—10/16.**G.**
Don. 10/3—28/5/21.**G.**
Don. 5/1—17/3/23.**H.**
Don. 24/10—22/12/23.**G.**
Don. 17/11/24—31/1/25.**H.**
Don. 6/8—13/11/26.**G.**
Don. 4/3—28/3/27.**L.**
Don. 18/10—23/12/27.**H.**
Don. 16/8—25/9/28.**G.**
Don. 14/3—18/4/31.**G.**
Cab sides altered.
Don. 26/11—24/12/32.**G.**
Don. 19/1—16/2/35.**G.**
Don. 7/11—28/11/36.**G.**
Don. 7/10—4/11/39.**G.**
Don. 4/9—18/9/43.**G.**
Don. 18/11—2/12/44.**G.**

BOILERS:
1327.
1372 1/05.
1380 11/11.
6848 10/16.
6925 17/3/23.
7109 23/12/27.
7276 18/4/31.
7535 *(superheated)* 16/2/35.
8284 18/9/43.

SHEDS:
Colwick.
South Lynn 24/11/36.
Yarmouth Beach 11/1/37.
King's Lynn 19/1/39.
Yarmouth Beach 15/3/39.
Norwich 12/11/39.
Yarmouth Beach 30/11/39.
Norwich 18/8/40.
Yarmouth Beach 19/10/40.
Norwich 19/12/41.
Melton Constable 11/4/42.
Norwich 23/4/42.
March 25/9/42.
Norwich 22/11/42.
Yarmouth Beach 28/3/43.
Melton Constable 17/10/43.
Yarmouth Beach 8/11/45.
Melton Constable 24/11/45.

RENUMBERED:
1327N 22/12/23.
4327 31/1/25.
2156 24/11/46.

CONDEMNED: 8/1/49.

4328

Doncaster 792.

To traffic 10/1898.

REPAIRS:
Don. ?/?—2/07.**G.**
Don. ?/?—11/12.**G.**
Don. 18/5—9/10/20.**G.**
Don. 27/8—13/12/24.**G.**
Don. 6/12/26—12/3/27.**G.**
Don. 6/4—18/5/29.**G.**
Cab sides altered.
Don. 27/2—2/4/32.**G.**
Don. 16/7—23/7/32.**L.**
Don. 18/5—8/6/35.**G.**

BOILERS:
1328.
1382 2/07.
1333 11/12.
6976 9/10/20.
D1885 *(new)* 12/3/27.
8829 *(superheated)* 8/6/35.

SHEDS:
Doncaster.
Colwick *by* 1927.
Leicester 24/9/30.
Colwick 9/5/31.
Retford 25/1/33.
Hitchin 7/6/35.
Lincoln 18/3/37.

RENUMBERED:
4328 13/12/24.

CONDEMNED: 22/10/37.

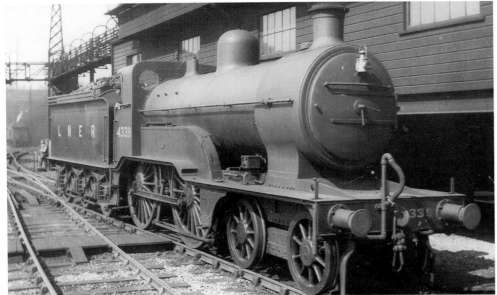

In November 1929 three more were superheated, Nos.4339, 4361 and 4392. They too had Ramsbottom safety valves. Retaining their flat valves and getting Hulburb type mechanical lubricator, they did not get the anti-carboniser.

Two more, Nos.4332 and 4382 were superheated in March 1930 and their newly built boilers had Ross 'Pop' safety valves. They too retained flat valves but got the Hulburb type mechanical lubricator, probably from those currently being replaced on the Pacifics by the No.7 Wakefield type.

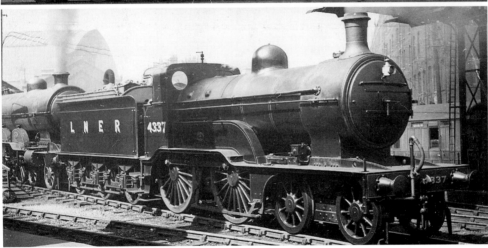

Between January 1935 and July 1937, fifteen more were superheated, got balanced slide valves, and were fitted with mechanical lubricator. The 1935 conversions were Nos.4327, 4328, 4330, 4337, 4338, 4365, 4367, 4377, 4379, 4387, 4391 and 3048. Nos.4363 and 4394 were done in 1936, and the last one, No.3050 was converted in July 1937 by which date withdrawals had already begun.

When new Nos.4321 to 4340 and 4361 to 4395 had taper shank buffers with solid spindle and some kept these to withdrawal. No.2190 (ex 4395) withdrawn in September 1949 was also still fitted with the frame on the tender for the A.R.P. blackout sheet used during the 1939-45 war to avoid glare from the firebox.

From 1905 there was a change to parallel shank with hollow spindle when new buffers were needed, and the fifteen engines built in 1907 and 1909 had that type when new.

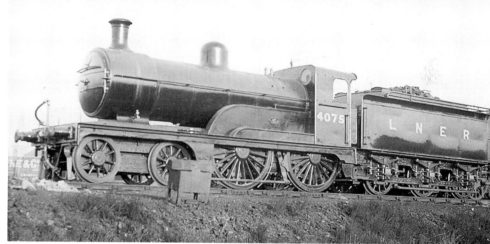

Nos.4321 to 4340 and 4361 to 4395 were originally fitted with plain flat coupling rods.

Nos.4396 to 4399, 4180 and 3041 to 3050 had fluted 'I' section coupling rods from when they were built. Most of the engines built earlier had their flat rods changed later to fluted type. However, a few did retain flat rods for many years, 4337 and 4387 still having them in 1936 whilst 4380 was recorded with them after its 1943 shopping.

Sanding was, and remained, steam operated for forward running, and gravity fed behind the leading coupled wheels was available for running tender first. The enamelled shed allocation plate (LINCOLN) can be seen inside the cab, under the roof.

4329

Doncaster 793.

To traffic 11/1898.

REPAIRS:
Don. ?/?—8/18.**G.**
Don. 5/10—20/11/20.**G.**
Don. 10/7—1/11/24.**G.**
Don. 19/2—22/5/6.**G.**
Don. 7/5—6/7/28.**G.**
Don. 11/10—8/11/30.**G.**
Cab sides altered.
Don. 24/6—22/7/33.**G.**
Don. 9/5—3/5/36.**G.**
Don. 19/2—5/3/38.**G.**
Don. 9/4/38.**L.**
Don. 29/11—27/12/41.**G.**
Don. 3/11—8/12/45.**G.**

BOLIERS:
1329.
6945 8/18.
7016 22/5/26.
8708 22/7/33.
8530 5/3/38.
9277 27/12/41.

SHEDS:
Colwick.
Leicester 10/5/34.
Colwick 13/9/35.
New England 4/12/36.
South Lynn 12/12/36.
March 29/1/39.
South Lynn 24/5/39.
Melton Constable ?/?
Yarmouth Beach 3/5/45.
Melton Constable 14/12/46.

RENUMBERED:
4329 1/11/24.
2157 3/11/46

CONDEMNED: 8/4/48.

4330

Doncaster 794.

To traffic 11/1898.

REPAIRS:
Don. ?/?—5/06.**G.**
Don. ?/?—3/09.**G.**
Don. ?/?—2/11.**G.**
Don. ?/?—7/18.**G.**
Don. 14/6—14/8/20.**G.**
Don. 6/11/23—1/3/24.**G.**
Don. 15/2—26/4/26.**G.**
Don. 3/3—23/8/28.**G.**
Don. 30/6—11/10/30.**G.**
Cab sides altered.
Don. 25/10—31/12/32.**G.**

Don. 15/3—11/5/35.**G.**
Don. 21/3—26/6/37.**G.**
Don. 28/9—2/12/39.**G.**
Don. 17/1—13/3/43.**G.**
Don. 27/2/46. Not repaired.

BOILERS:
1330.
1371 5/06.
1330 3/09.
1362 2/11.
1492 7/18.
6850 26/4/26.
7283 23/8/28.
7394 31/12/32.
8818 (superheated) 11/5/35.
8278 13/3/43.

SHEDS:
York.
Grantham 12/23.

RENUMBERED:
4330 1/3/24.
2158 allocated.

CONDEMNED: 29/3/46.
Cut up at Doncaster.

4331

Doncaster 795.

To traffic 11/1898.

REPAIRS:
Don. ?/?—5/03.**G.**
Don. ?/?—4/11.**G.**
Don. ?/?—5/18.**G.**
Don. 1/2—1/7/22.**G.**
Don. 1/7—9/10/26.**G.**
Don. 24/10—14/12/29.**G.**
Cab sides altered.
Don. 8/12/32—11/3/33.**G.**
Don. 14/8—28/9/35.**G.**
Don. 17/10—27/11/37.**G.**
Don. 7/9—12/10/40.**G.**
Don. 20/9—23/10/43.**G.**

BOILERS:
1331.
1493 5/03.
1492 4/11.
1371 5/18.
6945 9/10/26.
8467 11/3/33.
7475 27/11/37.
8329 12/10/40.

SHEDS:
York.
New England 12/1/25.
Boston ?/?
New England 2/2/28.
Grantham 8/9/33.

Boston 5/11/34.

RENUMBERED:
4331 27/1/25.
2159 23/10/46

CONDEMNED: 12/7/47.

4332

Doncaster 798.

To traffic 11/1898.

REPAIRS:
Don. ?/?—12/05.**G.**
Don. 17/5—18/9/20.**G.**
Don. 28/2—25/7/24.**G.**
Don. 15/5—29/8/25.**L.**
Don. 31/7—30/11/26.**G.**
Don. 19/11/27—2/2/28.**G.**
Don. 3/10/29—1/3/30.**G.**
Cab sides altered.
Don. 31/10/31—16/1/32.**G.**
Don. 21/9—3/11/34.**G.**
Don. 3/3—1/5/37.**G.**
Don. 9/9—21/10/39.**G.**
Don. 26/4—29/5/43.**G.**
Don. 10/12/45—2/2/46.**G.**
Don. 5/10/48. Not repaired.

BOILERS:
1332.
1368 12/05.
7110 18/9/20.
8276 (new; sup.htd) 1/3/30.
8828 21/10/39.

SHEDS:
Grantham
Boston 14/12/34.
Grantham 10/10/35.
Boston 14/3/36.
Hitchin 26/10/47.

RENUMBERED:
4332 25/7/24.
2160 17/2/46

CONDEMNED: 16/10/48.

4333

Doncaster 799.

To traffic 11/1898.

REPAIRS:
Don. ?/?—2/06.**G.**
Don. ?/?—8/14.**G.**
Don. 3/8—12/11/21.**G.**
Don. 10/12/23—3/5/24.**G.**
Don. 14/12/25—2/3/26.**G.**
Don. 18/6/28—26/1/29.**G.**
Don. 25/11/32—4/2/33.**G.**

Cab sides altered.
Don. 12/6—7/8/37.**G.**
Don. 29/9—26/10/40.**G.**
Don. 6/10—6/11/43.**G.**
Don. 30/6/50. Not repaired.

BOILERS:
1333.
1332 2/06.
1601 8/14.
7475 26/1/29.
8701 7/8/37.
9492 23/11/46.

SHEDS:
King's Cross (Hitchin).
Lincoln 4/3/37.
Louth 15/11/37.
Immingham 7/12/38.
Lincoln 6/1/39.
Retford 8/3/40.
Grantham 29/8/43.
Colwick 4/11/49.

RENUMBERED:
4333 3/5/24.
2161 8/4/46.

CONDEMNED: 10/7/50.
Cut up at Doncaster.

4334

Doncaster 800.

To traffic 11/1898.

REPAIRS:
Don. ?/?—12/04.**G.**
Don. ?/?—11/10.**G.**
Don. ?/?—8/17.**G.**
Don. 25/10/21—7/1/22.**G.**
Don. 5/1—26/3/25.**G.**
Don. 12/7—15/10/26.**G.**
Don. 30/1—31/5/28.**G.**
Don. 23/5—20/6/31.**G.**
Cab sides altered.
Don. 28/4—19/5/34.**G.**

BOILERS:
1334.
1380 12/04.
1371 11/10.
1380 8/17.
6932 7/1/22.
D1777 (new; sup.htd) 31/5/28.

SHEDS:
Doncaster.
New England by 4/24.
Boston 3/11/31.
New England 23/5/32.
Boston 5/11/34.

RENUMBERED:
4334 26/3/25.

CONDEMNED: 22/9/36.

4335

Doncaster 801.

To traffic 11/1898.

REPAIRS:
Don. ?/?—7/04.**G**.
Don. ?/?—3/06.**G**.
Don. ?/?—3/15.**G**.
Don. 28/2—6/7/22.**G**.
Don. 19/9—28/11/25.**G**.
Don. 22/9—23/11/28.**G**.
Don. 30/4—14/6/30.**G**.
Cab sides altered.
Don. 24/5—26/8/33.**G**.
Don. 31/12/35—1/2/36.**G**.
Don. 31/10—17/12/38.**G**.
Don. 23/2—26/4/41.**G**.
Don. 8—28/10/44.**G**.

BOILERS:
1335.
1339 7/04.
1331 3/06.
1372 3/15.
7644 6/7/22.
8386 14/6/30.
8704 17/12/38.

SHEDS:
Doncaster.
Boston *by* 4/24.
Grantham 27/9/34.
New England 13/10/36.
Peterborough East 3/12/36.
New England (MGN) 30/11/37.
New England 20/1/38.
New England (MGN) 19/2/38.
New England 4/6/39.
South Lynn 20/7/39.
New England 18/9/39.
New England (MGN) 11/5/43.
New England 27/8/44.
Colwick 16/4/45.

RENUMBERED:
4335 28/11/25.
2162 22/9/46.

CONDEMNED: 12/7/47.

4336

Doncaster 852.

To traffic 9/1899.

REPAIRS:
Don. ?/?—4/05.**G**.

Don. ?/?—5/11.**G**.
Don. ?/?—3/15.**G**.
Don. ?/?—8/19.**G**.
Don. 17/8—13/11/20.**G**.
Don. 2/4—5/9/24.**G**.
KXs. *Altered to G.E. gauge.*
Don. 4/10/26—8/1/27.**G**.
Don. 6/7—10/8/29.**G**.
Cab sides altered.
Don. 13/6—4/7/31.**G**.
Don. 13/1—10/2/34.**G**.
Don. 23/3—6/4/35.**L**.

BOILERS:
1336.
1601 4/05.
1495 5/11.
1366 3/15.
7405 8/19.
8196 10/8/29.
8190 10/2/34.

SHEDS:
Hitchin.
Ipswich 3/7/36.

RENUMBERED:
4336 5/9/24.

CONDEMNED: 6/5/37.

4337

Doncaster 853.

To traffic 10/1899.

REPAIRS:
Don. ?/?—12/05.**G**.
Don. ?/?—12/11.**G**.
Don. ?/?—7/19.**G**.
Don. 4/5—23/9/22.**G**.
Don. 6/11/24—21/2/25.**G**.
Don. 29/4—14/7/27.**G**.
Don. 13/2—22/3/30.**G**.
Cab sides altered.
Don. 10/12/32—28/1/33.**G**.
Don. 14/1—9/3/35.**G**.
Don. 4/6—31/7/37.**G**.
Don. 14/6—4/8/41.**G**.
Don. 8/10—10/11/45.**G**.
Don. 9/4/48. *Not repaired.*

BOILERS:
1337.
1324 12/05.
7057 12/11.
7410 7/19.
7996 14/7/27.
8815 *(superheated)* 9/3/35.

SHEDS:
Hitchin.
Retford 4/8/28.
Hitchin 10/6/35.

New England 2/9/43.
Boston 16/4/45.
Hitchin 26/10/47.

RENUMBERED:
4337 21/2/25.
2163 7/7/46.

CONDEMNED: 16/10/48.
Cut up at Doncaster.

4338

Doncaster 854.

To traffic 10/1899.

REPAIRS:
Don. ?/?—9/04.**G**.
Don. ?/?—9/08.**G**.
Don. 27/11/22—28/3/23.**G**.
Don. 2/3—30/5/25.**G**.
Don. 13/12/26—17/3/27.**G**.
Don. 25/3—10/8/29.**G**.
Cab sides altered.
Don. 31/8—24/10/31.**G**.
Don. 14/1—8/4/33.**G**.
Don. 1/1—23/2/35.**G**.
Don. 12/11—31/12/36.**G**.
Don. 5—15/2/37.**L**.
Don. 19/11/37—8/1/38.**G**.
Front heater connection fitted.
Don. 10/6—2/9/39.**G**.
Don. 4/4—8/5/43.**G**.

BOILERS:
1338.
1385 9/04.
1336 9/08.
6928 28/3/23.
8195 10/8/29.
8812 *(superheated)* 23/2/35.
8804 8/5/43.

SHED:
Grantham.

RENUMBERED:
4338 30/5/25.
2164 allocated.

CONDEMNED: 23/2/46.

4339

Doncaster 855.

To traffic 10/1899.

REPAIRS:
Don. ?/?—4/04.**G**.
Don. ?/?—11/08.**G**.
Don. ?/?—7/10.**G**.
Don. ?/?—10/11.**G**.
Don. 25/4—29/10/21.**G**.

Don. 6/9—20/11/23.**G**.
Don. 17/8—7/11/25.**G**.
Don. 6/6—23/8/27.**G**.
Don. 10/9—9/11/29.**G**.
Cab sides altered.
Don. 11/11—27/11/29.**N/C**.
Don. 23/10—19/12/31.**G**.
Don. 22/2—28/4/34.**G**.
Don. 25/6—22/8/36.**G**.
Don. 23/2—12/4/41.**G**.
Don. 22/10—16/12/41.**H**.
Don. 16/9—13/10/45.**G**.
Don. 28/2/49. *Not repaired.*

BOILERS:
1339.
1323 4/04.
1492 11/08.
1364 7/10.
1330 10/11.
7641 29/10/21.
7323 *(superheated)* 9/11/29.
7674 22/8/36.

SHEDS:
Grantham.
Colwick 28/11/29.
Hatfield 26/2/35.
Hitchin 6/9/36.
New England 21/6/40.

RENUMBERED:
1339N 20/11/23.
4339 7/11/25.
2165 17/11/46.

CONDEMNED: 18/3/49.
Cut up at Doncaster.

4340

Doncaster 856.

To traffic 10/1899.

REPAIRS:
Don. ?/?—2/05.**G**.
Don. ?/?—12/07.**G**.
Don. ?/?—8/11.**G**.
Don. 17/9/21—11/2/22.**G**.
Don. 23/2—9/5/25.**G**.
Don. 31/1—26/4/28.**G**.
Don. 24/11—31/12/30.**G**.
Cab sides altered.
Don. 26/5—28/7/34.**G**.
Don. 14/5—17/7/37.**G**.
Don. 24/9—18/11/39.**G**.
Don. 15/9—10/10/42.**G**.
Don. 12/1—29/1/44.**L**.
Don. 12/3—28/4/45.**G**.

BOILERS:
1340.
1370 2/05.
1375 12/07.

1337 8/11.
7755 9/5/25.
7471 31/12/30.
9202 18/11/39.

SHEDS:
King's Cross.
New England 26/4/28.
Retford 19/3/32.
New England 15/6/32.
Lincoln 6/11/34.
Immingham 19/2/36.
Lincoln 5/2/37.
Staveley 19/2/43
Colwick 9/8/43.

RENUMBERED:
4340 9/5/25.
2166 29/11/46.

CONDEMNED: 12/7/47.

4361

Doncaster 857.

To traffic 11/1899.

REPAIRS:
Don. ?/?—11/03.**G.**
Don. ?/?—10/09.**G.**
Don. ?/?—6/14.**G.**
Don. ?/?—10/19.**G.**
Don. 1/8/22—30/7/23.**G.**
Don. 14/5—17/10/25.**G.**
Don. 4/1—8/3/28.**G.**
Don. 4/9—2/11/29.**G.**
Don. 5/12—31/12/29.**G.**
Cab sides altered.
Don. 9/6—13/8/32.**G.**
Gor. 4/10—14/10/33.**L.**
Front heat connection fitted.
Don. 17/8—6/10/34.**G.**
Don. 28/2—11/4/38.**G.**
Don. 7/7—10/8/40.**G.**
Don. 2/9—25/9/43.**G.**
Don. 13/10—24/11/45.**G.**
Don. 24/1/49. *Not repaired.*

BOILERS:
1361.
1491 11/03.
1494 10/09.
1376 6/14.
6946 10/19.
7178 17/10/25.
7325 (*superheated*) 2/11/29.
8401 11/4/38.
7535 25/9/43.
8984 24/11/45.

SHEDS:
Colwick.
Trafford Park 19/9/32.
Colwick 12/10/32.

Heaton Mersey 26/1/33.
Trafford Park 13/4/34.
Heaton Mersey 13/7/35.
Hitchin 6/11/35.
Hornsey 17/4/36.
Grantham 25/1/37.

RENUMBERED:
4361 17/10/25.
2167 4/12/46.

CONDEMNED: 5/2/49.
Cut up at Doncaster.

4362

Doncaster 858.

To traffic 10/1899.

REPAIRS:
Don. ?/?—6/10.**G.**
Don. ?/?—8/16.**G.**
Don. 24/8—13/11/20.**G.**
Don. 12/7—11/10/24.**G.**
Don. 17/4—7/8/26.**G.**
Don. 5/1—16/2/29.**G.**
Don. 27/9—18/10/30.**G.**
Cab sides altered.
Don. 8/4—6/5/33.**G.**
Don. 8/9—22/9/34.**L.**
Don. 25/5—15/6/35.**G.**

BOILERS:
1362.
1370 6/10.
1599 8/16.
6865 11/10/24.
8187 16/2/29.
8703 6/5/33.

SHEDS:
Doncaster.
Colwick *by* 1/29.

RENUMBERED:
4362 11/10/24.

CONDEMNED: 24/6/37.

4363

Doncaster 859.

To traffic 10/1899.

REPAIRS:
Don. ?/?—2/05.**G.**
Don. ?/?—7/07.**G.**
Don. ?/?—1/15.**G.**
Don. 29/3—22/7/22.**G.**
Don. 2/10/24—10/1/25.**G.**
Don. 16/8—11/12/26.**G.**
Don. 6/4—4/5/29.**G.**
Don. 27/6—25/7/31.**G.**

Cab sides altered.
Don. 16/7—30/7/32.**L.**
Don. 7/4—28/4/34.**G.**
Don. 11/4—2/5/36.**G.**
Don. 25/12/37—15/1/38.**G.**
Don. 22/4/39. *Not repaired.*

BOILERS:
1363.
1326 2/05.
1414 7/07.
1332 1/15.
7637 22/7/22.
7406 4/5/29.
8940 (*superheated*) 2/5/36.

SHEDS.
Colwick.
New England 22/12/36.
Melton Constable 4/1/37.
South Lynn 11/1/37.

RENUMBERED:
4363 10/1/25.

CONDEMNED: 8/6/39.

4364

Doncaster 860.

To traffic 11/1899.

REPAIRS:
Don. ?/?—11/05.**G.**
Don. ?/?—5/13.**G.**
Don. 8/9/21—4/2/22.**G.**
Don. 13/10/24—17/1/25.**G.**
Don. 15/1—13/4/27.**G.**
Don. 26/1—6/4/29.**G.**
Don. 18/3—27/6/31.**G.**
Cab sides altered
Don. 24/4—29/7/33.**G.**
Don. 9/8—28/9/35.**G.**
Don. 15/12/37—8/1/38.**G.**
Don. 18/4—24/5/41.**G.**
Don. 2/11—27/11/43.**G.**
Don. 12/4—19/5/45.**G.**
Don. 1/5—1/6/46.**H.**
Don. 1/12/47. *Not repaired.*

BOILERS:
1364.
1376 11/05.
1378 5/13.
7059 4/2/22.
8193 6/4/29.
D1885 (*ex4328*) 28/9/35.
8336 24/5/41.
9146 19/5/45.
8537 1/6/46.

SHEDS:
Colwick
Leicester 12/5/36.

Colwick 23/7/37.
Leicester 15/3/38.
Colwick 28/2/41.
Botanic Gardens (*Book transfer*)
27/12/47.

RENUMBERED:
4364 17/1/25.
2168 19/12/46.

CONDEMNED: 27/12/47.
Cut up at Doncaster.

4365

Doncaster 861.

To traffic 11/1899.

REPAIRS:
Don. ?/?—3/05.**G.**
Don. ?/?—6/07.**G.**
Don. ?/?—5/10.**G.**
Don. 4/1—22/4/22.**G.**
Don. 1/10—27/12/24.**G.**
Don. 15/1—1/4/27.**G.**
Don. 23/2—4/5/29.**G.**
Don. 2/5—25/7/31.**G.**
Cab sides altered.
Don. 10/1—17/3/34.**G.**
Don. 11/1—9/3/35.**G.**
Don. 21/4—26/6/37.**G.**
Don. 28/8—21/10/39.**G.**
Don. 10/1—18/3/42.**G.**
Don. 7/5—10/6/44.**G.**
Don. 28/11/45—5/1/46.**H.**
Don. 21/4—16/5/47.**L.**

BOILERS:
1365.
1327 3/05.
1364 6/07.
1379 5/10.
7636 22/4/22.
7147 4/5/29.
8814 (*superheated*) 9/3/35.
9335 18/3/42.
7527 5/1/46.

SHEDS:
Leicester.
Colwick 27/12/24.

RENUMBERED:
4365 27/12/24.
2169 15/9/46.

CONDEMNED: 2/7/48.

4366

Doncaster 903.

To traffic 10/1900.

Until 1929 the cab cut-out was 2ft 10in. deep on all the cabs but was then considered to be too low for safety and comfort. Beginning with No.4393, ex works 1st June 1929, the cut-out was reduced by 9 inches and a hand grip in the cab side sheet was provided. All were so altered. Nos.4388 and 4396 in August 1933 being the last.

Until after the LNER took over, all (except No.1322) had built-up chimney 2ft 7¼in. high, giving 13ft 4⅛in. above rail level.

During October 1924, King's Cross shed fitted Nos.3041, 3042, 3049 and 4336 with 8in. shorter chimney - as used on J6 class - so that these engines could work excursions from Hatfield to the G.E. station at Southend-on-Sea.

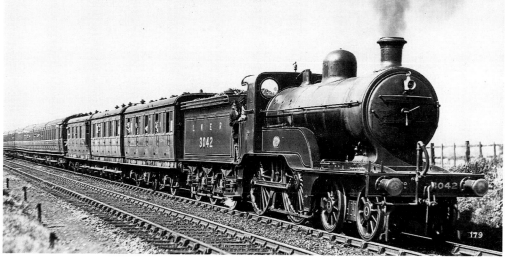

When ex works 17th April 1926, No.4377 had been fitted with a shorter built-up chimney of the type used on the 0-8-0 and 0-8-2T engines. Ten years later, on 4th July 1936, Doncaster fitted this same type to No.4366 which was then sent to Ipswich shed from Hitchin.

In the mid-1930's a number of those with tall chimney had 1½in. turned off the rim to allow restricted use on certain GE Section routes.

In 1936/7 several were fitted with J6 type chimney to allow unrestricted running on the GE Section, and from March 1939 all the survivors were so altered to clear GE gauge.

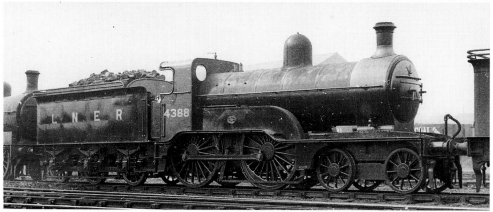

Originally the dome was 2ft 10in. high and covers to suit lasted at least until 1937.

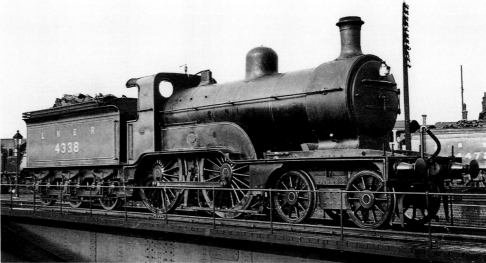

As early as 1908 dome height was reduced to 2ft 2in. and 8in. shorter covers could then be used and these presented no GE gauge problem.

From 1911 there was a further reduction of dome height on boilers used for D2 class to 1ft 11¼in. and covers were cut to suit. Originally 13ft 4¾in. over dome cover stud, this was cut to 12ft 4⅞in. in 1924 for engines selected to work on GE lines. From March 1939 all remaining engines had the dome cover reduced to the 12ft 4⅞in. height.

On all except the fifteen built in 1907/9 the boiler hand rails were pitched 4ft 5½in. above running plate level.

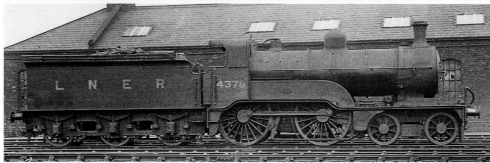

From about 1917 the standard height above running plate was made 4ft 0in. and gradual alteration to this was made.

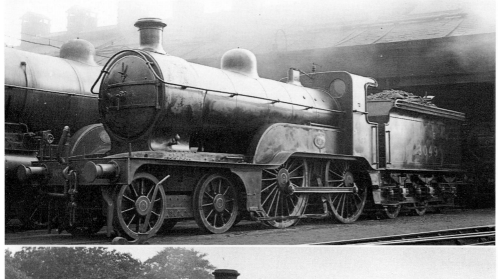

The last fifteen engines built also had continuous handrail but it was pitched 3 inches lower than on engines built previously. Nos.4387, 3049 and 3050 at least still had continuous rail after they got their 1924 numbers but were altered later.

From about 1911 the hand rails were cut to finish on the side of the smokebox but there were some exceptions. No.3049 had them cut to end on the smokebox front plate, and whilst No.1327N still had continuous rail, it did not have a cross rail until 1925. Cross rails also varied appreciably in length.

Until the replacement boilers built after the 1926 batch, the safety valves were Ramsbottom type with a cast iron cover.

There was then a change to Ross 'Pops' mounted directly on the firebox, but washout plugs were still fitted.

4366 continued.
REPAIRS:
Don. ?/?—1/06.**G.**
Don. ?/?—7/14.**G.**
Don. 26/4—24/9/21.**G.**
Don. 31/1—26/5/23.**G.**
Don. 20/7—17/10/25.**G.**
Don. 25/1—25/4/28.**G.**
Don. 23/5—20/6/31.**G.**
Cab sides altered.
Don. 20/6—4/7/36.**G.**
Chimney altered to G.E. gauge.
Don. 11/12—31/12/37.**G.**
Don. 27/7—24/8/40.**G.**
Don. 5/2—26/2/44.**G.**
Don. 9/3—16/3/46.**L.**

BOILERS:
1366.
1363 1/06.
6845 7/14.
7640 20/6/31.
8703 31/12/37.

SHEDS:
King's Cross.
Hitchin 1/11/35.
Ipswich 5/7/36.
Bury St Edmunds 11/6/38.
Cambridge 8/2/42.
South Lynn 14/4/42.
March 25/9/42.
South Lynn 17/5/43.
Norwich 5/8/43.
Melton Constable 6/10/43.
Yarmouth Beach 3/5/45.

RENUMBERED:
4366 1/25.
2170 15/3/46.

CONDEMNED: 25/8/47.

4367

Doncaster 904.

To traffic 10/1900.

REPAIRS:
Don. ?/?—10/05.**G.**
Don. ?/?—12/7/13.**G.**
Galloway-Hill furnace fitted.
Don. 16/3—31/5/18.**G.**
Don. 5/2—26/5/23.**G.**
G-H furnace removed.
Don. 1/2—16/4/26.**G.**
Don. 26/1—9/3/29.**G.**
Don. ?/?—7/6/32.**L.**
Cab sides altered.
Don. 24/12/32—21/1/33.**G.**
Don. 31/8—12/10/35.**G.**
Don. 13/5/39. *Not repaired.*

BOILERS:
1367.
1377 10/05.
1416 31/5/18.
8189 9/3/29.
8835 *(superheated)* 12/10/35.

SHEDS:
Boston.
New England 7/6/32.
Boston 23/10/33.
Grantham 25/9/34.
King's Cross 5/11/35.
Hornsey 29/11/35.
Hatfield 2/11/36.
King's Cross 6/12/36.
New England 14/3/37.
Lincoln 27/9/38.
Louth 28/9/38.

RENUMBERED:
4367 16/4/26.

CONDEMNED: 8/6/39.
Cut up at Doncaster.

4368

Doncaster 905.

To traffic 10/1900.

REPAIRS:
Don. ?/?—5/05.**G.**
Don. ?/?—4/07.**G.**
Don. ?/?—6/09.**G.**
Don. ?/?—12/11.**G.**
Don. ?/?—11/16.**G.**
Don. 12/10/21—18/2/22.**G.**
Don. 19/2—2/8/24.**G.**
Don. 19/12/25—10/3/26.**G.**
Don. 17/5/28—19/1/29.**G.**
Don. 11/3—13/6/31.**G.**
Cab sides altered.
Front heat connection fitted.
Don. 27/10/32—18/2/33.**G.**
Don. 2/10—23/11/35.**G.**
Don. 22/3—9/4/38.**L.**
Tablet catcher fitted.
Don. 13/7—12/8/40.**G.**
Don. 18/4—13/5/44.**G.**

BOILERS:
1368.
1335 5/05.
1379 4/07.
1361 6/09.
7061 12/11.
1600 11/16.
7394 19/1/29.
7283 18/2/33.
8193 23/11/35.

SHEDS:
Lincoln.
Louth 8/5/33.
Lincoln 27/5/33.
New England 3/11/34.
Peterborough East 11/1/37.
New England 2/11/37.
South Lynn 29/7/38.
New England 17/8/38.
New England MGN 19/2/39.
New England 2/6/41.
Boston 16/4/45.

RENUMBERED:
4368 2/8/24.
2171 8/746.

CONDEMNED: 3/4/47.

4369

Doncaster 906.

To traffic 10/1900.

REPAIRS:
Don. ?/?—3/06.**G.**
Don. ?/?—2/11.**G.**
Don. ?/?—7/17.**G.**
Don. 6/10—27/11/20.**G.**
Don. 20/6/22.**N/C.**
Don. 19/9—28/11/25.**G.**
Don. 24—30/6/27.**N/C.**
For balancing.
Don. 3/2—19/4/28.**G.**
Don. 21/3—24/5/30.**G.**
Cab sides altered.
Don. 11/4—6/8/32.**G.**
Don. 4—27/10/34.**G.**
Don. 8—10/12/34.**N/C.**
Don. 13/2—22/5/37.**G.**
Don. 20/11/39—20/1/40.**G.**
Don. 19/1—20/3/43.**G.**
Don. 16/11—15/12/45.**G.**
Don. 20/2—19/3/48.**G.**

BOILERS:
1369.
1339 3/06.
1384 2/11.
1369 7/17.
7052 28/11/25.
8536 6/8/32.
9353 20/3/43.

SHEDS:
Lincoln.
Louth 19/1/34.
Boston 5/8/37.
Grantham 26/10/47.
Colwick 18/5/49.

RENUMBERED:
4369 28/11/25.
2172 7/7/46.
62172 19/3/48.

CONDEMNED: 19/6/51.

4370

Doncaster 907.

To traffic 11/1900.

REPAIRS:
Don. ?/?—11/04.**G.**
Don. ?/?—6/05.**G.**
Don. ?/?—11/07.**G.**
Don. ?/?—10/09.**G.**
Don. ?/?—12/11.**G.**
Don. ?/?—6/16.**G.**
Don. 23/10/18—11/1/19.**G.**
Don. 8/10/23—9/2/24.**G.**
Don. 29/4—6/8/26.**G.**
Don. 30/8—27/10/28.**G.**
Don. 5/12/30—21/2/31.**G.**
Cab sides altered.
Don. 13/12/32—4/3/33.**G.**
Don. 1/8—21/9/35.**G.**
Don. 27/6—28/8/37.**G.**
Don. 28/4—1/6/40.**G.**
Don. 11/2—21/3/41.**L.**
Don. 18/9—16/10/43.**G.**
Don. 31/7—19/9/47.**G.**

BOILERS:
1370.
1324 11/04.
1375 6/05.
1335 11/07.
1365 10/09.
1600 12/11.
1365 6/16.
7003 9/2/24.
8411 21/2/31.
8466 28/8/37.
9006 19/9/47.

SHEDS:
Retford.
Lincoln 27/10/28.
Grantham 3/11/34.
Immingham 6/12/44.
Boston 16/4/45.
Grantham 26/10/47.
Colwick 3/10/48.

RENUMBERED:
1370N 9/2/24.
4370 20/3/25.
2173 20/10/46.

CONDEMNED: 29/5/50.

4371

Doncaaster 908.

To traffic 11/1900.

4371 continued.
REPAIRS:
Don. ?/?—1/06.**G**.
Don. ?/?—9/12.**G**.
Don. 18/12/20—30/4/21.**G**.
Don. 28/8—6/12/24.**G**.
Don. 26/10—19/12/25.**L**.
Don. 2/5—4/7/28.**G**.
Don. 2/4—30/4/32.**G**
Cab sides altered.
Don. 7/7—4/8/34.**G**.
Don. 28/3—18/4/36.**G**.
Don. 27/2—20/3/37.**G**.
Don. 3/2—2/3/40.**G**.
Don. 13/5—10/6/44.**G**.
Don. 21/8/47 *Not rep.*

BOILERS:
1371.
1340 1/06.
1361 9/12.
7013 6/12/24.
8528 30/4/32.
8194 18/4/36.

SHEDS:
Boston.
Colwick 12/9/32.
New England 22/12/36.
Melton Constable 4/1/37.
Norwich 23/9/38.
Melton Constable 26/11/38.
Norwich 29/1/39.
South Lynn 16/6/39.
March 9/2/41.
South Lynn 20/5/42.
Norwich 27/2/45.
Melton Constable 19/8/45.

RENUMBERED
4371 6/12/24.
2174 18/8/46.

CONDEMNED: 6/9/47.

4372

Doncaster 909.

To traffic 11/1900.

REPAIRS:
Don. ?/?—10/04.**G**.
Don. ?/?—10/06.**G**.
Don. 20/9—20/12/19.**G**.
Don. 5—30/12/22.**L**.
Don. 8/10/23—19/1/24.**G**.
Don. 3/2—24/4/26.**G**.
Altered to G.E. gauge.
Don. 1/12/28—19/1/29.**G**.
Don. 7—28/3/31.**G**.
Cab sides altered.
Don. 13/8—17/9/32.**G**.
Don. 23/12/33—27/1/34.**G**.
Don. 22/8—5/9/36.**G**.

BOILERS:
1372.
1322 10/04.
1367 10/06.
6923 20/12/19.
7276 19/1/29.
7998 28/3/31.
8466 17/9/32.
8528 5/9/36.

SHEDS:
York.
Sheffield 7/5/27.
King's Cross 29/10/27.
Hitchin ?/?
Hatfield 15/4/30.
Hitchin 26/2/35.
New England 25/5/36.
Ipswich 26/6/36.
New England 21/10/36.
Peterborough East 21/11/36.
New England MGN 10/6/38.

RENUMBERED:
4372 19/1/24.

CONDEMNED: 6/12/38.

4373

Doncaster 910.

To traffic 11/1900.

REPAIRS:
Don. ?/?—6/17.**G**.
Don. 11/4—1/8/22.**G**.
Don. 12/8—22/11/24.**G**.
Don. 2/3—7/5/27.**G**.
Don. 2/2—16/3/29.**G**.
Don. 21/3—18/4/31.**G**.
Cab sides altered.
Don. 3—24/6/33.**G**.
Don. 20/7—17/8/35.**G**.
Don. 30/4—14/5/38.**G**.
Don. 13/7—17/8/40.**G**.
Don. 26/6—31/7/43.**G**.
Don. 1/12/45—5/1/46.**G**.
Don. 5—12/10/46.**L**.

BOILERS:
1373.
6949 6/17.
6983 1/8/22.
7409 7/5/27.
8190 16/3/29.
8704 24/6/33.
8708 14/5/38.
8418 17/8/40.
9275 5/1/46.

SHEDS:
Colwick.
Sheffield 7/5/27.
Retford *by* 3/1/30.

Ipswich 9/9/36.
New England 10/12/36.
Melton Constable 18/12/36.
Norwich 10/5/42.
March 25/9/42.
Norwich 22/11/42.
Yarmouth Beach 8/8/43.

RENUMBERED:
4373 22/11/24.
2175 18/8/46.

CONDEMNED: 25/11/48.

4374

Doncaster 912.

To traffic 12/1900.

REPAIRS:
Don. ?/?—5/04.**G**.
Don. ?/?—7/15.**G**.
Don. ?/?—3/18.**G**.
Don. 1/7—18/9/20.**G**.
Don. 2/4—19/7/24.**G**.
Don. 23/4—14/7/26.**G**.
Don. 3/7—20/9/30.**G**.
Cab sides altered.
Don. 20/12/34—16/2/35.**G**.
Don. 22/8—18/9/37.**G**.
Don. 4/9—13/11/39.**G**.
Don. 25/9—23/10/43.**G**.
Don. 10/7/46. *Not repaired.*

BOILERS:
1374.
1325 5/04.
1323 7/15.
7008 3/18.
7471 14/7/26.
8387 20/9/30.
8411 18/9/37.
8531 13/11/39.
8391 23/10/43.

SHEDS:
Grantham.
Retford 15/1/25.
Hitchin 29/4/26.
Grantham 6/11/35.
Boston 21/5/36.
New England 24/11/36.
Peterborough East 5/12/36.
New England MGN 16/10/37.
Peterborough East 26/10/37.
New England MGN 24/11/37.
New England 2/6/41.
Colwick 16/4/45.
Staveley 21/10/45.
Colwick 11/11/45.

RENUMBERED:
4374 19/7/24.
2176 22/7/46.

CONDEMNED: 1/1/47.
Cut up at Doncaster.
In store 27/9/30—11/7/31.

4375

Doncaster 916.

To traffic 12/1900.

REPAIRS:
Don. ?/?—2/05.**G**.
Don. ?/?—11/14.**G**.
Don. 6/7—15/10/21.**G**.
Don. 18/3—2/8/24.**G**.
Don. 22/10/26—22/1/27.**G**.
Don. 29/1—27/4/29.**G**.
Don. 27/7—26/9/31.**G**.
Cab sides altered.
Don. 20/7—7/10/33.**G**.
Don. 21/12/35—18/1/36.**G**.
Don. 4/5—11/6/38.**G**.
Don. 26/9/39. *Not repaired.*

BOILERS:
1375.
1602 2/05.
1324 11/14.
7638 15/10/21.
8194 27/4/29.
8189 18/1/36.
8394 11/6/38.

SHEDS:
Colwick.
Hitchin 4/10/33.
Retford 4/1/35.
Ipswich 8/9/36.
New England 17/12/36.
Melton Constable 19/12/36.
Yarmouth Beach 29/12/36.

RENUMBERED:
4375 2/8/24.

CONDEMNED: 9/12/39.
Cut up at Doncaster.

4376

Doncaster 917.

To traffic 12/1900.

REPAIRS:
Don. ?/?—3/05.**G**.
Don. ?/?—1/11.**G**.
Don. 23/5—19/11/21.**G**.
Don. 18/11/24—21/2/25.**G**.
Don. 25/3—22/4/27.**G**.
Don. 17/8—25/10/27.**G**.
Don. 21/9—19/10/29.**G**.
Cab sides altered.
Don. 2/4—7/5/32.**G**.
Don. 4—25/11/33.**G**.

Boilers built from December 1935 had two handholes instead of three plugs, and at first were fitted with domed cover plates. Wartime maintenance problems caused the handhole covers to be discarded and none were to be seen after 1945.

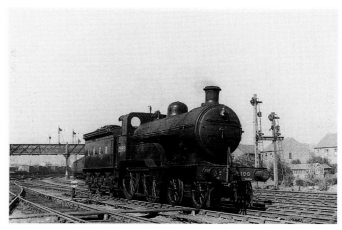

By no means did all post-war survivors have the front end heater connection fitted. Note that No.2199 still had Ramsbottom safety valves to its 18th July 1949 withdrawal.

During the 1930's some had front end carriage heating connection put on. Note that in this May 1938 photograph No.3046 still had a full length chimney.

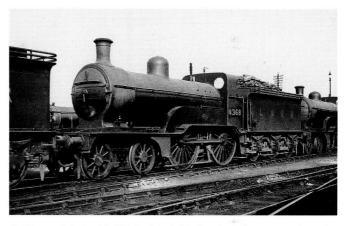

4368 was fitted with Whittaker tablet exchanging apparatus at a light repair, ex works 9th April 1938. At least thirteen D2's were fitted from early 1937 with a tablet exchanger for use on M&GN line workings, those recorded were: 3042, 3045, 3046, 4321, 4322, 4327, 4329, 4368, 4372, 4373, 4374, 4376, 4394. Note that for the M&GN workings only the rim of the original tall chimney needed removal. Note also the stop fitted to prevent the smokebox door swinging too far open. This was only fitted from 1932 onwards.

This facility for tender first running was still available after the war. No.4377 was re-numbered 2177 on 11th August 1946 but the job was not completed at the front end.

Boilers built to 1931 had the vacuum ejector exhaust pipe through the boiler itself but replacement boilers thereafter had the pipe placed outside the boiler along the right hand side as on 4337 here which appears to be in winter storage.

There were five different tender types coupled to D2 class. This was a Class A as introduced by Ivatt in 1896 for his 4-4-0 engines. Those with a water scoop had a capacity of 3140 gallons.

This was the 1903 modification to a Class A tender with altered front end, but without the hand grip fitted. Axles were still equally spaced at 6ft 6in. and 6ft 6in. apart.

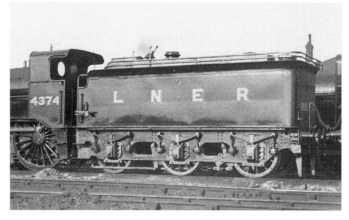

Class B tenders were similar to the 1903 Class A variety except that they had a 500 gallon well tank which put their water capacity to 3670 gallons. Only the early Class B with equal axle spacing was used with D2 class.

From 1905 the handgrip was added and the axle spacing became 6ft 10½in. and 6ft 1½in for new tenders.

In their early years some had Stirling design tenders of Class D which had three coal rails and a wooden buffer beam. Only Nos.4336 and 4338 were noted with this type in early LNER years, but during the 1939-45 war, there may have been some temporary couplings.

4376 continued.
Don. 6—27/4/35.**G.**
Don. 30/11—14/12/35.**L.**

BOILERS:
1376.
1600 3/05.
1374 1/11.
7753 21/2/25.
8530 7/5/32.

SHEDS:
Copley Hill.
Lincoln ?/?
New England 4/12/36.
South Lynn 12/12/36.
King's Lynn 30/9/37.

RENUMBERED:
4376 21/2/25.

CONDEMNED: 2/11/37.

4377

Doncaster 918.

To traffic 1/1901.

REPAIRS:
Don. ?/?—3/05.**G.**
Don. ?/?—1/16.**G.**
Don. 4/4—23/7/21.**G.**
Don. 14—24/12/21.**L.**
Don. 3/3—20/9/24.**G.**
Don. 2/2—17/4/26.**G.**
Altered to G.E. gauge.
Don. 22/10/27—3/1/28.**G.**
Don. 31.5—28/7/29.**G.**
Cab sides altered.
Don. 11/8—17/10/31.**G.**
Don. 8/6—30/7/32.**G.**
Don. 16/11/34—12/1/35.**G.**
Don. 27/2—22/5/37.**G.**
Don. 18/9—18/10/42.**G.**
Don. 29/3—26/5/45.**G.**
Don. 16/12/45—19/1/46.**L.**
Don. 17/11—19/12/47.**G.**
Don. 19/9/49. *Not repaired.*

BOILERS:
1377.
1338 3/05.
1602 1/16.
7076 17/4/26.
7737 *(superheated)* 12/1/35.
8547 19/12/47.

SHEDS:
King's Cross (Hatfield).
King's Cross.
Lincoln 5/1/28.
Louth 25/10/28.
Lincoln 13/1/32.
Louth 7/11/35.

Hitchin 9/12/35.
Frodingham 13/11/38.
Doncaster 20/2/40.
New England 31/10/42.
Immingham 6/12/44.
Colwick 20/1/46.

RENUMBERED:
4377 20/9/24.
2177 11/8/46.

CONDEMNED: 3/10/49.
Cut up at Doncaster.

4378

Doncaster 919.

To traffic 1/1901.

REPAIRS:
Don. ?/?—3/04.**G.**
Don. ?/?—7/05.**G.**
Don. ?/?—4/09.**G.**
Don. ?/?—2/19.**G.**
Don. 16/1—19/5/23.**G.**
Don. 20/10/25—30/1/26.**G.**
Don. 1/12/27—23/2/28.**G.**
Don. 18/1—15/2/30.**G.**
Cab sides altered.
Don. 4/3—1/4/33.**G.**
Gor. 1—8/7/33.**L.**
Front heater connection fitted.

BOILERS:
1378.
1331 3/04.
1365 7/05.
1385 4/09.
7401 2/19.
D1747 *(new: sup.htd)* 23/2/28.

SHEDS:
Doncaster.
Trafford Park 31/3/33.
King's Cross 31/8/35.
Hornsey 17/4/36.
King's Cross 25/7/36.
Hatfield 6/9/36.

RENUMBERED:
4378 17/2/25.

CONDEMNED: 18/6/37.

4379

Doncaster 920.

To traffic 1/1901.

REPAIRS:
Don. ?/?—7/06.**G.**
Don. ?/?—1/15.**G.**
Don. 5/7—23/11/22.**G.**

Don. 20/4—18/7/25.**G.**
Don. 13/2—24/8/28.**G.**
Don. 30/10—31/12/31.**G.**
Cab sides altered.
Don. 11/1—23/2/35.**G.**
Don. 14/10—3/12/38.**G.**
Don. 17/8—18/9/43.**G.**
Don. 21/10—9/11/43.**L.**
Don. 8/4—19/5/45.**G.**

BOILERS:
1379.
1366 7/06.
1363 1/15.
7533 24/8/28.
7747 *(superheated)* 23/2/35.

SHEDS:
Boston.
Grantham 8/12/34.
Peterborough East 9/10/35.
New England 6/1/36.
Boston 23/11/36.
New England 18/12/36.
New England MGN 7/7/40.
New England 25/5/41.
New England MGN 11/5/43.
New England 27/8/44.
Immingham 6/12/44.
Frodingham 23/12/45.

RENUMBERED:
4379 18/7/25.
2178 8/9/46.

CONDEMNED: 28/7/47.

4380

Doncaster 911.

To traffic 11/1900.

REPAIRS:
Don. ?/?—4/04.**G.**
Don. ?/?—11/08.**G.**
Don. ?/?—5/16.**G.**
Don. 18/1—3/6/22.**G.**
Don. 17/2—9/5/25.**G.**
Don. 13/2—5/4/28.**G.**
Don. 26/3—4/7/31.**G.**
Cab sides altered.
Don. 21/10/33—27/1/34.**G.**
Don. 4/11—15/12/36.**G.**
Don. 9/6—8/7/40.**G.**
Don. 29/6—25/7/43.**G.**
Don. 10/12/45—19/1/46.**G.**
Don. 30/1/49. *Not repaired.*

BOILERS
1380.
1361 4/04.
1326 11/08.
1494 5/16.
7643 3/6/22.

8413 4/7/31.
7998 15/12/36.
8330 25/7/43.

SHEDS:
Boston.
Retford 26/1/34.
Staveley 4/1/37.
Retford 25/6/37.
Grantham 29/8/43.
Boston 4/5/47.

RENUMBERED:
4380 9/5/25.
2179 15/7/46.

CONDEMNED: 1/3/49.
Cut up at Doncaster.

4381

Doncaster 921.

To traffic 1/1901.

REPAIRS:
Don. ?/?—12/09.**G.**
Don. ?/?—18/4/14.**G.**
Don. 15/3—25/5/19.**G.**
Don. 27/9—22/12/23.**G.**
Don. 29/4—15/10/26.**G.**
Don. 21/4—19/7/28.**G.**
Don. 18/4—29/7/30.**G.**
Cab sides altered.
Don. 23/9—26/11/32.**G.**
Don. 15/1—9/2/35.**G.**
Don. 1/2—20/3/37.**G.**
Don. 18/9—11/11/39.**G.**
Don. 1—14/12/40.**L.**
Don. 27/12/41—2/2/42.**L.**
Don. 16/2—24/4/43.**G.**
Don. 1—18/3/44.**G.**
Don. 29/5—12/8/47.**G.**

BOILERS:
1381.
1419 12/09.
6931 *(superheated)* 18/4/14.
8397 29/7/30.
8940 24/4/43.
8829 18/3/44.

SHEDS:
Retford.
Heaton Mersey 23/1/33.
Trafford Park 19/4/34.
Boston 26/6/35.

RENUMBERED:
1381N 22/12/23.
4381 17/3/25.
2180 14/7/46.

CONDEMNED: 1/5/50.

4382

Doncaster 913.

To traffic 11/1900.

REPAIRS:
Don. ?/?—11/05.**G.**
Don. ?/?—4/10.**G.**
Don. ?/?—2/19.**G.**
Don. 30/3—26/8/22.**G.**
Don. 18/2—16/5/25.**G.**
Don. 14/7—14/10/27.**G.**
Don. 25/1—1/3/30.**G.**
Cab sides altered.
Front heater connection fitted.
Don. 9—23/7/32.**G.**
Don. 19/5—23/6/34.**G.**
Don. 11/1—1/2/36.**G.**

BOILERS:
1382.
1374 11/05.
1383 4/10.
7403 2/19.
8279 *(new; sup.htd)* 1/3/30.

SHEDS:
Boston.
Lincoln.
Louth 25/10/28.

RENUMBERED:
4382 16/5/25.

CONDEMNED: 15/5/37.

4383

Doncaster 914.

To traffic 12/1900.

REPAIRS:
Don. ?/?—10/05.**G.**
Don. ?/?—7/16.**G.**
Don. 16/9/21—25/1/22.**G.**
Front heater connection fitted at
Louth shed 3/24.
Don. 23/9/25—16/1/26.**G.**
Don. 1/12/28—2/2/29.**G.**
Don. 27/7—26/9/31.**G.**
Cab sides altered.
Don. 16/5—9/9/33.**G.**
Don. 4/10—9/11/35.**G.**
Don. 31/1—5/3/38.**G.**
Don. 17/9—19/10/40.**G.**
Don. 19/7—28/8/43.**G.**
Don. 17/9/46—29/8/47.**G.**

BOILERS:
1383.
1334 10/05.
6846 7/16.
7271 16/1/26.

7751 9/9/33.
8334 5/3/38.
7998 28/8/43.
9354 29/8/47.

SHEDS:
Louth.
Boston 5/8/37.

RENUMBERED
4383 16/1/26.
2181 17/7/46.

CONDEMNED: 20/11/50.

4384

Doncaster 915.

To traffic 12/1900.

REPAIRS:
Don. ?/?—2/10.**G.**
Don. ?/?—6/14.**G.**
Don. 14/6—20/9/19.**G.**
Don. 12/2—2/6/23.**G.**
Don. 9/8—20/11/26.**G.**
Don. 25/5—13/7/29.**G.**
Cab sides altered.
Don. 12/10—31/12/31.**G.**
Don. 23/8—29/9/34.**G.**
Don. 3/2—5/3/38.**G.**
Don. 28/11—21/12/40.**G.**
Don. 12/10—13/11/43.**G.**
Don. 24/2/46. *Not repaired.*

BOILERS:
1384.
1491 2/10.
6930 6/14.
7409 20/9/19.
D1888 *(new)* 20/11/26.
D1873 29/9/34.
8188 *(ex 4393)* 5/3/38.

SHED:
Boston.

RENUMBERED:
4384 7/2/25.
2182 allocated.

CONDEMNED: 29/3/46.
Cut up at Doncaster.

4385

Doncaster 922.

To traffic 12/1900.

REPAIRS:
Don. ?/?—8/04.**G.**
Don. ?/?—2/13.**G.**
Don. 20/7—30/10/20.**G.**

Don. 3/3—19/7/24.**G.**
Don. 3/8—10/11/26.**G.**
Don. 26/3—20/7/29.**G.**
Cab sides altered.
Don. 28/11/31—27/2/32.**G.**
Don. 4/5—23/6/34.**G.**
Don. 15/12/36—30/1/37.**G.**
Don. 22/5—29/7/39.**G.**
Don. 28/5—16/7/42.**G.**
Don. 23/8—19/9/43.**H.**

BOILERS:
1385.
1378 8/04.
1417 2/13.
1368 30/10/20.
1336 19/7/24.
7397 10/11/26.
7639 27/2/32.
8706 29/7/39.
9001 16/7/42.
8334 19/9/43.

SHEDS:
Hitchin.
King's Cross 14/7/33.
Leicester 4/8/33.
King's Cross 19/8/33.
Colwick 9/9/33.
Retford 19/12/34.
Boston 27/1/37.

RENUMBERED:
4385 19/7/24.
2183 14/7/46.

CONDEMNED: 12/7/47.

4386

Doncaster 975.

To traffic 1/1903.

REPAIRS:
Don. ?/?—3/07.**G.**
Don. ?/?—1/09.**G.**
Don. ?/?—11/10.**G.**
Don. 10/2—1/5/20.**G.**
Don. 24/4—1/9/23.**G.**
Don. 11/5—24/8/27.**G.**
Don. 20/4—1/6/29.**G.**
Cab sides altered.
Don. 14/3—11/4/31.**G.**
Don. 25/6—2/7/32.**G.**
Don. 9—30/6/34.**G.**
Don. 11/3/39. *Not repaired.*

BOILERS:
1412.
1369 3/07.
1337 1/09.
1321 11/10.
7007 1/5/20.
7142 1/6/29.

SHEDS:
Doncaster.
York 12/23.
Waskerley 17/5/35.
York 17/7/35.
Botanic Gardens 1/6/37.

RENUMBERED:
1386N 1/9/23.
4386 24/4/25.

CONDEMNED: 16/3/39.
Cut up at Doncaster.

4387

Doncaster 981.

To traffic 2/1903.

REPAIRS:
Don. ?/?—1/09.**G.**
Don. ?/?—7/11.**G.**
Don. ?/?—7/13.**G.**
Don. ?/?—2/18.**G.**
Don. 1/3—14/5/21.**G.**
Don. 2/11/23—23/2/24.**G.**
Don. 4/8—20/11/26.**G.**
Don. 29/11—20/12/30.**G.**
Cab sides altered.
Don. 28/9—26/10/35.**G.**
Don. 26/9—10/10/36.**G.**
Don. 19/9—8/10/38.**L.**
Don. 4/2—18/3/39.**L.**
Don. 19/1—16/3/40.**G.**
Don. 18/1—12/2/44.**G.**
Don. 27/4—18/5/46.**L.**
Don. 5—14/10/46.**H.**
Don. 8/11/47. *Not repaired.*

BOILERS:
1416.
1417 1/09.
1421 7/11.
1418 7/13.
1326 2/18.
7148 23/2/24.
D1880 *(new)* 20/11/26.
8837 *(superheated)* 26/10/35.
8804 *(ex4338)* 14/10/46.

SHEDS:
Doncaster.
York 12/23.
Botanic Gardens 6/6/39.

RENUMBERED:
4387 23/2/24.
2184 8/9/46.

CONDEMNED: 27/12/47.
Cut up at Doncaster.

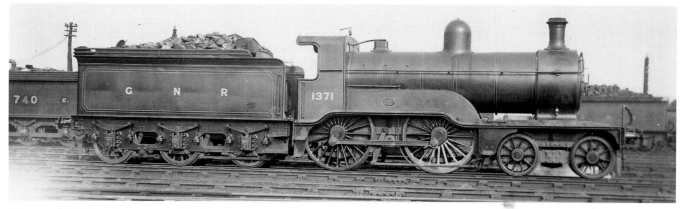

When the LNER took over the whole class had the GNR lined green passenger livery.

Until the June 1928 economies, green livery was continued for D2 class. Whilst L&NER was used to the middle of June 1923 it was put on ten D2 class: 45, 47, 48, 1326, 1327, 1338, 1366, 1367, 1378, 1384. Ex works 16th June 1923, No.1321 had the new livery without the ampersand and No.1361 (*see* page 39) out on 30th July was lettered similarly.

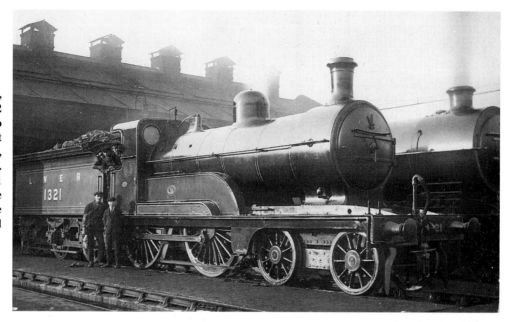

Beginning with No.1386, ex works 1st September 1923, the area suffix N was added to the number and was applied to nine D2: 1305 (29/10/23), 1323 (19/1/24), 1339 (20/11/23), 1370 (9/2/24), 1381 (22/12/23), 1386 (1/9/23), 1392 (13/10/23), 1395 (20/10/23), 1397 (10/11/23). A tenth engine, No.1327, also got the suffix; ex Doncaster 17th March 1923 following a heavy repair and boiler change, it was painted LNER green with lettering L&NER. It returned to Doncaster for a General in the following October and came out from that on 22nd December, still letter L&NER but now with the N suffix.

The N suffix was discarded from early February 1924 and it was painted out on 1386's tender, leaving the number off centre. This was probably due to the engine's transfer to York shed in December 1923.

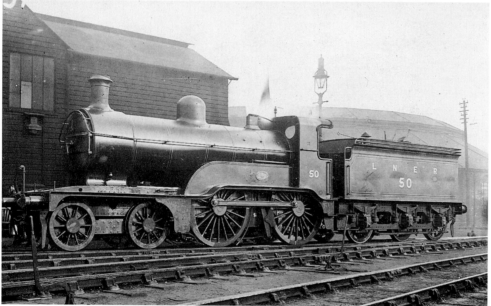

No.50 was not shopped at Doncaster works between 12th October 1922 and 30th October 1924 and the engine remained in GNR painting with number on the cab side. As this photograph was taken on 6th November 1923 it seems to have had a tender change and a re-painting by King's Cross shed.

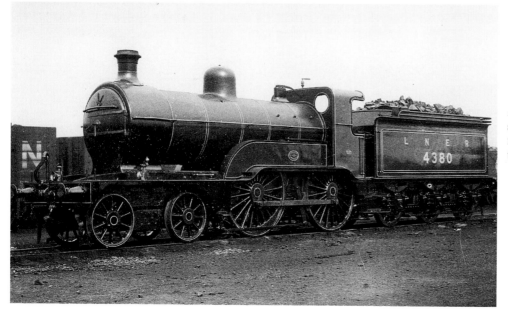

All the others not mentioned went straight to LNER green with numbers increased by 3000 and this style was used to 1928.

4388

Doncaster 977.

To traffic 2/1903.

REPAIRS:
Don. ?/?—5/07.**G.**
Don. ?/?—8/09.**G.**
Don. ?/?—11/16.**G.**
Don. 12/8—23/10/20.**G.**
Don. 21/3—9/8/24.**G.**
Don. 21/7—15/10/26.**G.**
Don. 19/9—31/10/28.**G.**
Don. 8/5—12/8/33.**G.**
Cab sides altered.
Don. 13/3—29/5/37.**G.**
Don. 3/3—12/4/41.**G.**
Don. 12/1—5/2/44.**G.**

BOILERS:
1414.
1383 5/07.
1369 8/09.
1335 11/16.
D1895 *(new)* 15/10/26.
7993 12/8/33.
8880 *(exJ5 3033)* 5/2/44.

SHEDS:
Doncaster *at* 1/22.
Hitchin *by* 12/22.
King's Cross 5/11/28.
Boston 8/2/35.

RENUMBERED:
4388 9/8/24.
2185 28/7/46.

CONDEMNED: 12/7/47.

4389

Doncaster 980.

To taffic 2/1903.

REPAIRS:
Don. ?/?—8/13.**G.**
Don. 17/8—25/11/22.**G.**
Don. 30/6—6/9/24.**G.**
Don. 7/6—9/10/26.**G.**
Don. 18/5—22/6/29.**G.**
Cab sides altered.
Don. 31/3—21/4/34.**G.**

BOILERS:
1415.
6847 8/13.
6872 25/11/22.
7415 9/10/26.
D1895 *(ex4388)* 21/4/34.

SHEDS:
Hitchin.

King's Cross 10/6/28.
New England 9/1/35.
Boston 17/4/35.

RENUMBERED:
4389 6/9/24.

CONDEMNED: 21/4/37.

4390

Doncaster 990.

To traffic 5/1903.

REPAIRS:
Don. ?/?—12/11.**G.**
Don. ?/?—10/19.**G.**
Don. 22/6—18/11/22.**G.**
Don. 11/12/24—14/3/25.**L.**
Don. 7/4—31/7/26.**G.**
Don. 12/7/28—12/1/29.**G.**
Don. 24/4—18/7/31.**G.**
Cab sides altered.
Don. 9/7—18/8/34.**G.**
Don. 21/8—18/9/37.**G.**
Don. 30—31/3/39.**N/C.**
Don. 20/11—21/12/40.**G.**
Don. 27/9—30/10/43.**G.**
Don. 22/2—17/3/45.**L.**
Don. 17/4/47. *Not repaired.*

BOILERS:
1420.
1412 12/11.
7406 10/19.
7284 12/1/29.
8413 18/9/37.

SHEDS:
York.
Doncaster 6/1/25.
New England 31/10/42.
Immingham 8/7/45.
Retford 23/12/45.
New England 10/3/46.

RENUMBERED:
4390 14/3/25.
2186 9/8/46.

CONDEMNED: 20/5/47.
Cut up at Doncaster.

4391

Doncaster 979.

To traffic 6/1903.

REPAIRS:
Don. ?/?—5/08.**G.**
Don. ?/?—10/10.**G.**
Don. ?/?—2/16.**G.**
Don. 2/8—18/11/22.**G.**

Don. 12/1—11/4/25.**G.**
Don. 24/3—11/6/27.**G.**
Don. 12/3—9/4/32.**G.**
Cab sides altered.
Don. 30/3—18/5/35.**G.**
Don. 23/1—6/2/37.**G.**

BOILERS:
1413.
1412 5/08.
1335 10/10.
1421 2/16.
7103 11/6/27.
8828 *(superheated)* 18/5/35.

SHEDS:
King's Cross.
Hitchin 26/11/32.
Colwick 22/8/33.
Louth 10/6/37.

RENUMBERED:
4391 11/4/25.

CONDEMNED: 25/8/38.

4392

Doncaster 994.

To traffic 4/1903.

REPAIRS:
Don. ?/?—6/11.**G.**
Don. ?/?—1/13.**G.**
Don. 1/12/20—16/4/21.**H.**
Don. 11/8—8/10/21.**L.**
Don. 26/7—9/9/22.**L.**
Don. 29/5—13/10/23.**G.**
Don. 5/12/24—14/2/25.**G.**
Don. 8/4—29/6/27.**G.**
Don. 21/9—16/11/29.**G.**
Cab sides altered.
Don. 15/1—9/4/32.**G.**
Gor. 4—14/10/33.**L.**
Front heater connection fitted.
Don. 26/6—18/8/34.**G.**
Don. 22/11—14/12/35.**L.**
Don. 1/11—19/12/36.**G.**
Don. 9/7—20/8/38.**G.**
Don. 21/8—10/11/39.**L.**
Don. 30/5—7/7/41.**G.**
Don. 27/12/43—29/1/44.**G.**
Don. 30/3—28/4/45.**L.**
Don. 30/5—7/7/45.**L.**
Don. 23/4—22/6/46.**G.**
Don. 29/8/48. *Not repaired.*

BOILERS:
1421.
1493 6/11.
1420 1/13.
7010 13/10/23.
7414 *(superheated)* 16/11/29.
D1771 *(exJ6 3590)* 19/12/36.

8711 22/6/46.

SHEDS:
Lincoln.
Immingham 6/1/27.
Lincoln 23/7/27.
Colwick 28/11/29.
Heaton Mersey 26/1/33.
Trafford Park 26/5/33.
Heaton Mersey 13/7/35.
Hitchin 12/11/35.
Louth 10/12/35.
Colwick 29/8/43.

RENUMBERED:
1392ₙ 13/10/23.
4392 14/2/25.
2187 6/10/46.

CONDEMNED: 1/10/48.
Cut up at Doncaster.

4393

Doncaster 995.

To traffic 2/1903.

REPAIRS:
Don. ?/?—10/08.**G.**
Don. ?/?—9/18.**G.**
Don. 23/3—6/8/21.**G.**
Don. 30/1—23/8/24.**G.**
Don. 28/10/26—2/2/27.**G.**
Don. 12/2—1/3/27.**L.**
Don. 6/4—1/6/29.**G.**
Cab sides altered.
Don. 8/8—10/10/31.**G.**
Don. 11/1—24/3/34.**G.**
Don. 10—21/3/36.**G.**
Don. 18/3—21/5/38.**G.**
Don. 1/12/39—20/1/40.**G.**
Don. 7—23/5/42.**G.**
Don. 16/5—17/6/44.**G.**
Don. 20/3—4/5/46.**H.**
Don. 5/1—11/2/48.**G.**
Don. 12/9/49. *Not repaired.*

BOILERS:
1417.
1328 10/08.
1418 9/18.
6849 6/8/21.
D1873 *(new)* 2/2/27.
7757 24/3/34.
D1873 *(ex4384)* 21/5/38.
8391 20/1/40.
9276 23/5/42.
9630 4/5/46.

SHEDS:
Colwick.
Langwith Jct 17/9/41.
Colwick 6/11/41.

RENUMBERED:
4393 22/8/24.
2188 6/10/46.
E**2188** 11/2/48.

CONDEMNED: 3/10/49.
Cut up at Doncaster.

4394

Doncaster 992.

To traffic 5/1903.

REPAIRS:
Don. ?/?—6/09.**G.**
Don. ?/?—4/15.**G.**
Don. 28/10/21—22/4/22.**G.**
Don. 10/11/24—7/2/25.**G.**
Don. 21/2—10/7/28.**G.**
Don. 28/2—21/3/31.**G.**
Cab sides altered.
Don. 17/3—14/4/34.**G.**
Don. 15/2—14/3/36.**G.**
Don. 14/10—18/11/39.**G.**
Don. 6—27/3/43.**G.**
Don. 29/5—10/7/43.**L.**
Don. 19/2—11/3/44.**L.**
Don. 2—10/11/46.**G.**

BOILERS:
1419.
1323 6/09.
1491 4/15.
7279 10/7/28.
8938 (superheated) 14/3/36.

SHEDS:
Boston.
Lincoln 3/11/34.
New England 4/12/36.
South Lynn 12/12/36.
March 1/10/37.
South Lynn 30/6/38.
King's Lynn 25/11/39.
South Lynn 9/6/40.
March 9/2/41.
South Lynn 20/5/42.
Melton Constable 8/2/45.

RENUMBERED:
4394 7/2/25.
2189 18/8/46.

CONDEMNED: 25/11/48.

4395

Doncaster 993.

To traffic 3/1903.

REPAIRS:
Don. ?/?—4/13.**G.**
Don. ?/?—1/18.**G.**

Don. 3/3—22/5/20.**G.**
Don. 24/5—20/10/23.**G.**
Don. 30/7—10/11/26.**G.**
Don. 25/3—18/5/29.**G.**
Cab sides altered.
Don. 20/5—25/7/31.**G.**
Don. 3/3—5/5/34.**G.**
Don. 18/5—27/6/36.**G.**
Don. 28/12/38—4/2/39.**G.**
Don. 15/6—23/7/41.**G.**
Don. 1/2—2/3/42.**L.**
Don. 29/12/43—22/1/44.**G.**
Don. 27/10/46—28/6/47.**G.**
Don. 19/8/49. Not repaired.

BOILERS:
1418.
1339 4/13.
1384 1/18.
7057 22/5/20.
7002 10/11/26.
8328 5/5/34.
7994 27/6/36.
8876 22/1/44.

SHEDS:
Boston.
Woodford 21/5/29.
Boston 3/7/29.
New England 26/10/47.
Colwick 3/10/48.

RENUMBERED:
1395N 20/10/23.
4395 10/11/26.
2190 28/7/46.

CONDEMNED: 5/9/49.
Cut up at Doncaster.

4396

Doncaster 1165.

To traffic 8/1907.

REPAIRS:
Don. ?/?—4/14.**G.**
Don. 14/3—29/4/22.**L.**
Don. 17/12/23—7/6/24.**G.**
Don. 15/9—31/12/26.**G.**
Don. 6/10—24/11/28.**G.**
Don. 1/7—12/8/33.**G.**
Cab sides altered.
Don. 10/2—3/3/34.**G.**

BOLIERS:
6845.
1419 4/14.
7149 7/6/24.
6872 31/12/26.
8706 12/8/33.

SHEDS:
Doncaster.

York 12/23.
Malton 14/7/31.
York 17/12/31.

RENUMBERED:
4396 7/6/24.

CONDEMNED: 2/8/38.

4397

Doncaster 1167.

To traffic 8/1907.

REPAIRS:
Don. ?/?—10/15.**G.**
Don. 19/1—16/3/18.**G.**
Don. 9/8—10/11/23.**G.**
Don. 14/7—31/10/25.**G.**
Don. 7/12/25.**L.**
Don. 18/2—11/5/28.**G.**
Don. 25/4—18/6/30.**G.**
Cab sides altered.
Don. 30/4—18/6/32.**G.**
Don. 21/5—14/7/34.**G.**
Don. 20—21/7/34.**L.**
Tender changed.
Don. 9/5—13/6/36.**G.**
Don. 18/10/38. Not repaired.

BOILERS:
6846.
1325 10/15.
7011 31/10/25.
8531 18/6/32.

SHEDS:
Doncaster.
Lincoln 3/11/28.
Louth 10/8/31.
Immingham 2/2/37.
Colwick 19/7/37.

RENUMBERED:
1397N 10/11/23.
4397 31/10/25.

CONDEMNED: 4/11/38.
Cut up at Doncaster.

4398

Doncaster 1169.

To traffic 10/1907.

REPAIRS:
Don. ?/?—2/13.**G.**
Don. ?/?—11/17.**G.**
Don. 22/3—25/6/21.**G.**
Don. 17/12/23—17/5/24.**G.**
Don. 15/6—2/9/26.**G.**
Don. 9—30/11/29.**G.**
Cab sides altered.

Don. 21/10—11/11/33.**G.**
Don. 11—24/12/37.**G.**
Don. 20/3—1/5/43.**G.**
Don. 12/6/47. Not repaired.

BOILERS:
6847.
1340 2/13.
1370 11/17.
7105 17/5/24.
7641 30/11/29.
8000 11/11/33.
8467 24/12/37.

SHEDS:
Doncaster.
York 12/23.
Botanic Gardens 15/7/37.
Neville Hill 30/5/40.
Botanic Gardens 17/8/40.

RENUMBERED:
4398 17/5/24.
2191 15/9/46.

CONDEMNED: 28/6/47.
Cut up at Doncaster.

4399

Doncaster 1169.

To traffic 9/1907.

REPAIRS:
Don. ?/?—9/15.**G.**
Don. 15/5—11/11/22.**G.**
Don. 20/4—8/8/25.**G.**
Don. 13/12/27—4/5/28.**G.**
Don. 17/6—23/8/30.**G.**
Cab sides altered.
Don. 8/2—20/5/33.**G.**
Don. 9/3—27/4/35.**G.**
Don. 11/4—14/6/37.**G.**
Don. 12/3—16/4/38.**G.**
Don. 23/7—1/10/38.**L.**
Don. 30/8—12/10/40.**G.**
Don. 15/5—10/6/44.**G.**
Don. 16/4/46. Not repaired.

BOILERS:
6848.
1493 9/15.
7241 (superheated) 4/5/28.
8567 14/6/37.
8939 10/6/44.

SHEDS:
Colwick.
Trafford Park 16/5/33.
Peterborough East 26/8/35.
Grantham 9/10/35.
New England 24/4/40.
New England MGN 8/6/41.
New England 27/8/44.

RENUMBERED:
4399 8/8/25.
2192 allocated.

CONDEMNED: 18/5/46.
Cut up at Doncaster.

4180

Doncaster 1170.

To traffic 9/1907.

REPAIRS:
Don. ?/?—2/15.**G.**
Don. 3/6—22/10/21.**G.**
Don. 4/9—12/12/24.**L.**
Don. 5/11/27—13/1/28.**G.**
Don. 19/3—9/4/32.**G.**
Cab sides altered.
Don. 7—28/7/34.**G.**
Don. 17/6—5/8/39.**G.**
Don. 14/8—4/9/43.**G.**
Don. 20/5—10/6/44.**L.**
Don. 2—9/9/44.**G.**
Don. 5—19/1/46.**L.**
Don. 28/8—11/10/47.**G.**

BOILERS:
6849.
7059 2/15.
7642 22/10/21.
8419 9/4/32.
8530 *(exJ5 3024)* 9/9/44.

SHEDS:
York.
Botanic Gardens 1/6/37.
Colwick 28/12/47.

RENUMBERED:
4180 12/12/24.
2193 1/12/46.

CONDEMNED: 20/6/49.

3041

Doncaster 1226.

To traffic 3/1909.

REPAIRS:
Don. ?/?—8/13.**G.**
Don. ?/?—8/19.**G.**
Don. 21/3—8/7/22.**G.**
Don. 18/2—16/8/24.**G.**
KXs. 9/24. *Short chimney and*
dome to G.E. gauge fitted.
Don. 29/4—23/7/27.**G.**
Don. 18/2—8/6/29.**G.**
Cab sides altered.
Front heater connection fitted.
Don. 18/12/30—23/2/31.**G.**
Don. 8/2—6/5/33.**G.**

Don. 14/12/34—19/1/35.**G.**
Don. 31/10—28/11/36.**G.**
Don. 5/9—4/11/39.**G.**
Don. 25/4—5/6/43.**G.**
Don. 13/3—13/4/46.**G.**
Don. 6/10—16/11/47.**G.**

BOILERS:
6930.
7060 8/13.
7408 8/19.
7998 23/7/27.
7004 23/2/31.
7754 19/1/35.
8528 4/11/39.
8411 5/6/43.
9352 16/11/47.

SHEDS:
King's Cross (Hatfield).
Lincoln 28/12/36.
Grantham 29/8/43.
Immingham 26/1/45.
Colwick 6/1/46.

RENUMBERED:
3041 16/8/24.
2194 13/4/46.

CONDEMNED: 22/6/49.

3042

Doncaster 1227.

To traffic 3/1909.

REPAIRS:
Don. ?/?—10/13.**G.**
Don. 4/5—27/8/21.**G.**
Don. 2/11/23—1/3/24.**G.**
KXs. 9/24. *Short chimney and*
dome to G.E. gauge fitted.
Don. 18/5—8/8/25.**G.**
Don. 10/8—18/10/27.**G.**
Don. 28/9—26/10/29.**G.**
Cab sides altered.
Don. 16/5—13/6/31.**G.**
Don. 4/3—1/4/33.**G.**
Don. 27/10—17/11/34.**G.**
Don. 26/12/36—16/1/37.**G.**
Don. 18/12—24/12/37.**L.**
Don. 27/4—18/5/40.**G.**
Str. 27/10/41.**L.**
Don. 30/10—20/11/43.**G.**
Don. 1—29/9/45.**G.**

BOILERS:
6931.
1415 10/13.
6984 27/8/21.
6952 1/3/24.
8000 18/10/27.
8469 1/4/33.
8415 16/1/37.

9274 29/9/45.

SHEDS:
King's Cross (Hatfield).
Ipswich 3/7/36.
New England 13/1/37.
South Lynn 6/2/37.
Yarmouth Beach 23/2/37.
Norwich 3/1/38.
Yarmouth Beach 30/5/38.
Norwich 29/9/38.
Yarmouth Beach 12/6/39.
Melton Constable 13/6/41.
Norwich 7/1/42.
Melton Constable 21/3/43.

RENUMBERED:
3042 1/3/24.
2195 8/12/46

CONDEMNED: 26/2/48.

3043

Doncaster 1228.

To traffic 3/1909.

REPAIRS:
Don. 3/5—3/9/21.**G.**
Don. 4/3—27/9/24.**G.**
Don. 10/8—26/9/25.**G.**
Don. 29/11/26—11/2/27.**G.**
Don. 25/5—29/6/29.**G.**
Cab sides altered.
Don. 31/1—7/3/31.**G.**
Don. 1—29/7/33.**G.**
Don. 7/9—12/10/35.**G.**
Don. 4/6/38. *Not repaired.*

BOILERS:
6932.
6981 3/9/21.
6868 27/9/24.
D1881 *(new)* 11/2/27.
8192 29/7/33.

SHEDS:
Copley Hill.
Grantham 9/2/26.

RENUMBERED:
3043 27/9/24.

CONDEMNED: 16/6/38.

3044

Doncaster 1229.

To traffic 4/1909.

REPAIRS:
Don. 11/1—21/4/22.**G.**
Don. 14/10/24—3/1/25.**G.**

Don. 30/6—1/10/27.**G.**
Don. 23/5—13/7/29.**G.**
Cab sides altered.
Don. 20/6—5/9/31.**G.**
Don. 2/6—19/8/33.**G.**
Don. 15/8—5/10/35.**G.**
Don. 7/2—5/3/38.**G.**
Don. 5/5—3/6/40.**G.**
Don. 29/6—31/7/43.**G.**
Don. 7—17/9/43.**N/C.**
Don. 18/9—13/10/45.**G.**
Don. 12/4/47. *Not repaired.*

BOILERS:
6933.
7639 21/4/22.
8414 5/9/31.
7405 5/3/38.
7754 3/6/40.
8732 31/7/43.

SHEDS:
Copley Hill.
Grantham 1924.
Immingham 2/2/45.
Retford 23/12/45.
Grantham 10/3/46.

RENUMBERED:
3044 3/1/25.
2196 5/1/47.

CONDEMNED: 20/5/47.
Cut up at Doncaster.

3045

Doncaster 1230.

To traffic 4/1909.

REPAIRS:
Don. ?/?—6/18.**G.**
Don. 12/8—9/10/20.**G.**
Don. 27/2—12/5/23.**G.**
Don. 6/11/25—27/2/26.**G.**
Don. 25/9—9/11/28.**G.**
Don. 24/10—21/11/31.**G.**
Cab sides altered.
Don. 12/5—16/6/34.**G.**
Don. 5—26/9/36.**G.**
Don. 12/11—31/12/38.**G.**
Don. 14/1—18/2/39.**L.**
Don. 3/6—22/7/39.**H.**
Don. 22/4—13/5/44.**G.**
Don. 21/8—26/9/47.**G.**
Don. 5/1/49. *Not repaired.*

BOILERS:
6934.
6978 6/18.
7102 12/5/23.
7643 21/11/31.
9490 *(new)* 13/5/44.

3045 continued.
SHEDS:
Boston.
Grantham 18/6/34.
Boston 3/11/34.
South Lynn 18/7/39.
King's Lynn 19/10/39.
South Lynn 9/6/40.
Cambridge 9/2/41.
South Lynn 14/4/42.
Yarmouth Beach 25/7/43.
Melton Constable 16/4/44.

RENUMBERED:
3045 *by* 7/25.
2197 21/12/46.

CONDEMNED: 8/1/49.
Cut up at Doncaster.

3046

Doncaster 1231.

To traffic 4/1909.

REPAIRS:
Don. ?/?—6/18.**G.**
Don. 28/4—30/7/21.**G.**
Don. 13/5—11/10/24.**G.**
Don. 14/3—21/5/27.**G.**
Don. 7/9—12/10/29.**G.**
Cab sides altered.
Don. 20/8—24/9/32.**G.**
Don. 18/1—8/2/36.**G.**
Don. 29/5—5/6/37.**L.**

BOILERS:
6945.
6874 6/18.
7057 21/5/27.
7402 12/10/29.

SHEDS:
Lincoln.
New England 3/11/34.
Peterborough East 23/10/35.
Boston 1/1/36.
New England 23/11/36.
Peterborough East 11/12/36.
New England 29/9/38.

RENUMBERED:
3046 11/10/24.

CONDEMNED: 4/11/38.

3047

Doncaster 1232.

To traffic 5/1909.

REPAIRS:
Don. ?/?—10/15.**G.**
Don. 8/4—14/4/20.**L.**
Don. 22/1—16/6/23.**G.**
Don. 29/6—17/10/25.**G.**
Don. 2/3—19/5/28.**G.**
Don. 16/9—15/11/30.**G.**
Cab sides altered.
Don. 31/7—21/9/35.**G.**
Don. 23/7—14/8/37.**G.**
Don. 25/12/39—10/2/40.**G.**
Don. 30/6—9/8/41.**G.**
Don. 12/12/42—2/1/43.**G.**
Don. 25/11—16/12/44.**G.**
Don. 24/2—11/4/47.**G.**
Don. 3/8/48. *Not repaired.*

BOILERS:
6947.
1495 10/15.
7058 17/10/25.
8388 15/11/30.
8469 14/8/37.
9005 16/12/44.

SHEDS:
York.
Doncaster 12/23.
Colwick 16/8/33.

RENUMBERED:
3047 17/10/25.
2198 22/12/46.

CONDEMNED: 27/8/48.
Cut up at Doncaster.

3048

Doncaster 1233.

To traffic 5/1909.

REPAIRS:
Don. 11/1—19/4/19.**G.**
Don. 8/11/22—17/3/23.**G.**
Don. 25/9—28/11/25.**G.**
Don. 12/11/26—14/1/27.**G.**
Don. 1/3—17/10/28.**G.**
Don. 14/9—15/11/30.**G.**
Cab sides altered.
Don. 3/12/30—16/8/33
In store.
Don. 15/8—5/10/35.**G.**
Don. 3/10—6/11/37.**G.**

Don. 2/12/39—20/1/40.**G.**
Don. 28/10/41—13/1/42.**G.**
Don. 7/6—8/7/44.**G.**
Don. 18/3—27/4/46.**G.**
Don. 6/10—5/11/47.**G.**
Don. 12/7/49. *Not repaired.*

BOILERS:
6946.
7404 19/4/19.
D1755 *(exJ6 3554; superheated)*
5/10/35.
8940 20/1/40.
8404 13/1/42.
D1765 *(exN1 4602)* 27/4/46.

SHEDS:
York.
Doncaster 12/23.
Colwick 16/8/33.

RENUMBERED:
3048 16/3/25.
2199 27/4/46.

CONDEMNED: 18/7/49.
Cut up at Doncaster.

3049

Doncaster 1234.

To traffic 5/1909.

REPAIRS:
Don. ?/?—2/19.**G.**
Don. 12/10/21—14/1/22.**G.**
Don. 26/5—25/10/24.**G.**
KXs. 11/24.**L.**
Fitted with short chimney &
dome for G.E. gauge.
Don. 15/2—30/4/27.**G.**
Don. 14/9—2/11/29.**G.**
Cab sides altered.
Don. 8/11/29—6/6/30.**N/C.**
Stored.
Don. 2/12/32—4/3/33.**G.**
Don. 9/8—5/10/35.**G.**
Don. 25/8—12/10/40.**G.**
Don. 1—28/3/44.**G.**
Don. 13/7/46. *Not repaired.*

BOILERS:
6948.
7013 2/19.
6981 25/10/24.
7752 4/3/33.

SHEDS:
Hitchin.
New England 1/8/40.

Hitchin 14/8/43.
Boston 2/1/44.

RENUMBERED:
3049 25/10/24.
2200 7/7/46.

CONDEMNED: 27/7/46.
Cut up at Doncaster.

3050

Doncaster 1235.

To traffic 5/1909.

REPAIRS:
Don. ?/?—4/17.**G.**
Don. 29/3—12/10/22.**G.**
Don. 30/10/24—14/2/25.**G.**
Don. 24/3—11/6/27.**G.**
Don. 9/10—7/12/29.**G.**
Cab sides altered.
Don. 26/1—15/4/33.**G.**
Don. 9/6—31/7/37.**G.**
Don. 5/5—10/7/39.**G.**
Don. 5/9—27/10/41.**G.**
Don. 31/10—28/11/42.**G.**
Don. 24/4—30/5/44.**G.**
Don. 11—27/1/45.**L.**

BOILERS:
6949.
7061 4/17.
7148 11/6/27.
9057 *(superheated)* 31/7/37.
8695 30/5/44.

SHEDS:
Hitchin.
Sheffield 23/2/34.
Retford 24/2/34.
Hitchin 23/3/34.
Colwick 21/11/35.

RENUMBERED:
3050 14/2/25.
2201 15/12/46.

CONDEMNED: 12/7/47.

WORKS CODES:- Cw - Cowlairs. Dar- Darlington. Dfu - Dunfermline shed. Don - Doncaster. Ghd - Gateshead. Gor - Gorton. Inv - Inverurie. Str - Stratford.
REPAIR CODES:- **C/H** - Casual Heavy. **C/L** - Casual Light. **G** - General. **H** - Heavy. **H/I** - Heavy Intermediate. **L** - Light. **L/I** - Light Intermediate. **N/C** - Non-Classified.

No.4305 was ex works 25th June 1928 in black with single red lining which was used until 1941.

On 1st June 1929 Doncaster were still turning out engines with numbers on tenders but they then began to put them on the cab and all the class were duly altered. The standard then became 12in. LNER on the tender, but the restricted width of the D2 cab side sheet only allowed 9in. numbers to be used. Not all seem to have had lining. From June 1942 until January 1946 only NE was put on the tender and none had lining put on after November 1941.

LNER was put on the tender from January 1946 and whilst stocks lasted the usual shaded transfers were used. From April 1947, yellow painted unshaded 12in. Gill sans letters were put on the tender. On the cab 9in. figures continued to be used although now 12in. size could have been accommodated. the figures were not true Gill sans as the 6 and 9 had been modified.

After a spate of repairs in the last months of the LNER only two more were carried out. On 11th February 1948 No.E2188 was out with 10in. Gill sans letters and numbers, and with regional letter above the number, both on the cab side and buffer beam.

Finally No.62172 was out on 19th March 1948 with full BR number and Doncaster found no difficulty in putting five 10in. numbers on the cabside. Again the modified 6 was included.

At the front, No.62172 had its number on the buffer beam, none got a smokebox plate. This engine did however acquire a BR cast shed plate 38A showing its allocation to Colwick, as here on 17th June 1951. Two days later, as the last of class, it was withdrawn nearly fifteen years since the first of the class to go, No.4334, which had been withdrawn in September 1936.

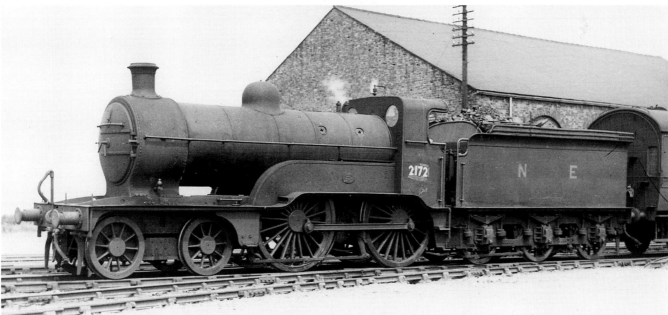

(*above*) The 1946 renumbering was very varied in style according to where it was done. No.4369 became 2172 on Sunday 7th July 1946 at Boston shed where 8½in. stencilled figures were not very skilfully applied.

No.4398 was altered to 2191 by Hull Botanic Gardens shed on Sunday 15th September 1946 and they not only found shaded transfers, but showed that 12in. figures could be used, albeit with two '1's' in the make-up. Although 2184, 2191 and 2193 were N.E. Area engines, they all got the J6 type chimney and shorter dome for which there was no need in their case.

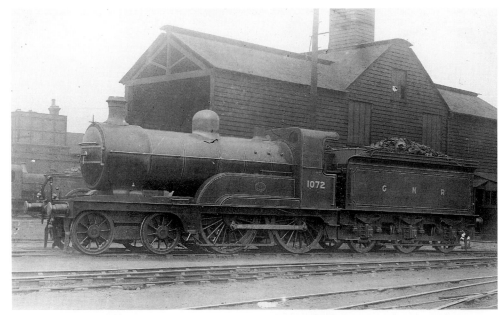

During 1913, five more D4's, Nos.1072, 1305, 1306, 1317 and 1354, got the bigger boiler and 2ft 2¼in. chimney. These engines included the straight running plate variety.

The next one re-boilered, No.1316 in February 1914 had the sandboxes for reverse running put in the cab, and the feed pipes moved to the rear instead of the front coupled wheels. As a result, No.1316 got separate splashers, but was the only one of the 51 engines so altered. Between July 1914 and April 1921 a further 38 received the 4ft 8in. boiler but without any alteration to splashers and sanding. Like No.1316 however they were fitted with the 2ft 7¼in. chimney.

At Grouping, only six, Nos.4077, 4079, 4313, 4356, 4358 and 4360 remained to re-boiler and they were dealt with between June 1923 and June 1928.

CLASS D3 & D4

3400

Doncaster 712.

To traffic 12/1896.

REPAIRS:
Don. ?/?—7/02.**G**.
Don. ?/?—3/09.**G**.
Don. ?/?—18/9/20.**G**.
Rebuilt to D3.
Don. 17/4—7/7/23.**G**.
Don. 19/3—20/6/25.**G**.
Don. 4/8—13/10/27.**G**.
Don. 2—23/11/29.**G**.
Cab sides altered.
Don. 18/6—9/7/32.**G**.
Don. 3—24/11/34.**G**.
Don. 15/1—5/2/44.**G**.
Don. 29/8/47. *Not repaired.*

BOILERS:
 400.
1298 7/02.
6919 3/09.
7492 18/9/20.
7852 20/6/25.
7662 9/7/32.

SHEDS:
Colwick.
New England 23/2/37.
New England MGN. 1/3/37.
New England 10/11/37.
South Lynn 29/7/38.
New England 16/8/38.
South Lynn 20/7/39.
New England 18/9/39.
March 22/9/39.
South Lynn 9/6/40.
Cambridge 9/2/41.
March 20/9/42.
South Lynn 17/7/43.

RENUMBERED:
3400 20/6/25.
2115 18/8/46.

CONDEMNED: 6/9/47.
Cut up at Doncaster.

4071

Doncaster 723.

To traffic 5/1897.

REPAIRS:
Don. ?/?—11/08.**G**.
Don. ?/?—15/12/17.**G**.
Rebuilt to D3.

Don. 23/3—17/6/22.**G**.
Don. 20/11/24—21/2/25.**G**.
Don. 23/6—11/10/27.**G**.
Don. 26/10—23/11/29.**G**.
Cab sides altered.
Don. 5/11—3/12/32.**G**.
Don. 6—20/11/37.**G**.
Don. 21—26/2/38.**L**.
Don. 16/11/42—3/1/43.**G**.
Don. 21/2—10/3/45.**L**.
Don. 25/11/45—5/1/46.**G**.
Don. 23/9/48. *Not repaired.*

BOILERS:
1071.
6887 11/08.
7372 1512/17.
7355 11/10/27.
7661 23/11/29.
8640 3/12/32.

SHEDS:
York.
Colwick 14/1/25.
Darlington 6/7/33.
York 9/10/34.
Doncaster 8/11/37.
Lincoln 5/3/38.
New England 27/7/38.
Lincoln 27/9/38.
Retford 8/3/40.
Immingham 9/8/43.
Retford 10/3/46.
Boston 8/6/47.
Colwick 14/9/47.

RENUMBERED:
4071 21/2/25.
2116 18/8/46.

CONDEMNED: 16/10/48.
Cut up at Doncaster.

4072

Doncaster 724.

To traffic 5/1897.

REPAIRS:
Don. ?/?—5/04.**G**.
Don. ?/?—12/4/13.**G**.
Rebuilt to D3.
Don. 5/1—1/4/22.**G**.
Don. 11/10/24—24/1/25.**G**.
Don. 12/8—21/10/27.**G**.
Don. 18/1—15/2/30.**G**.
Cab sides altered.
Don. 17/9—8/10/32.**G**.

BOILERS:
1072.
1451 5/04.
7155 12/4/13.
7299 1/4/22.
7352 21/10/27.

SHEDS:
Hitchin.
Immingham 28/10/27.
Lincoln ?/?
Louth 28/4/34.

RENUMBERED:
4072 24/1/25.

CONDEMNED: 20/12/35.

4073

Doncaster 725.

To traffic 6/1897.

REPAIRS:
Don. ?/?—8/02.**G**.
Don. ?/?—8/06.**G**.
Don. ?/?—7/14.**G**.
Don. ?/?—29/4/16.**G**.
Rebuilt to D3.
Don. 10/10/21—11/3/22.**G**.
Don. 2/4—16/8/24.**G**.
Don. 11/12/26—31/3/27.**G**.
Don. 8/9—2/11/29.**G**.
Cab sides altered.
Don. 8/11/29—6/6/30.**N/C**.
Tallowed down for storage.
Don. 27/7—30/9/33.**G**.
Don. 30/4—18/6/38.**G**.
Don. 12/3—19/4/41.**G**.
Don. 16/1/46. *Not repaired.*

BOILERS:
1073.
1299 8/02.
6808 8/06.
1435 7/14.
7308 29/4/16.
7314 16/8/24.
8451 30/9/33.
7853 18/6/38.

SHEDS:
Hitchin.
Colwick 22/11/35.
Leicester 27/8/37.
Colwick 26/9/37.
Hitchin 1/9/43.

RENUMBERED:
4073 16/8/24.
2117 allocated.

CONDEMNED: 23/2/46.
Cut up at Doncaster.

4074

Doncaster 726.

To traffic 6/1897.

REPAIRS:
Don. ?/?—3/05.**G**.
Don. ?/?—8/10.**G**.
Don. ?/?—17/2/17.**G**.
Rebuilt to D3.
Don. 6/12/22—27/1/23.**G**.
Don. 8/8—22/11/24.**G**.
Don. 13/11/26—10/2/27.**G**.
Don. 20/10—7/12/29.**G**.
Cab sides altered.
9/12/29—6/6/30.**N/C**.
Tallowed down for storage.
Don. 3/6—3/9/32.**G**.
Don. 30/3—20/4/35.**G**.
Don. 3—27/8/38.**G**.
Don. 14/11—11/12/43.**G**.
Don. 16/6/46. *Not repaired.*

BOILERS:
1074.
1075 3/05.
6989 8/10.
7353 17/2/17.
D1893 *(new)* 10/2/27.
D1897 *(exJ3 4166)* 20/4/35.
7445 27/8/38.
8054 11/12/43.

SHEDS:
Retford.
Sheffield 4/7/28.
Retford 10/9/28.
Sheffield 8/7/29.
Retford 21/9/29.
Botanic Gardens 8/7/35.
Colwick 23/10/35.
Neasden 15/1/40.
New England 24/6/40.
Grantham 28/9/42.
Immingham 19/8/43.

RENUMBERED:
4074 22/11/24.
2118 18/8/46.

CONDEMNED: 2/11/46.
Cut up at Doncaster.

4075

Doncaster 727.

To traffic 6/1897.

REPAIRS:
Don. ?/?—6/02.**G**
Don. ?/?—10/06.**G**.
Don. ?/?—5/8/16.**G**.
Rebuilt to D3.
Don. 25/10/21—24/2/22.**L**.
Don. 18/8—12/12/24.**G**.
Don. 23/4—29/7/27.**G**.
Don. 14/12/29—11/1/30.**G**.
Cab sides altered.
Dar. 10—26/12/30.**L**.
Raven F.S.A fitted.
Dar. 9/3—8/4/31.**L**.
After collision at Starbeck.
Dar. 20—22/5/31.**N/C**.
Don. 10/6—5/8/32.**G**.
Don. 3/2—10/3/34.**G**.
Don. 16/5—22/6/35.**G**.
S.W. Cab fitted.
Don. 8—27/11/37.**G**.
Don. 15/6—21/7/41.**G**.
Don. 6/9—14/10/44.**G**.
Don. 27/10—20/11/44.**L**.
For painting.
Don. 19/1/46.**N/C**.
Don. 13/9—24/10/47.**G**.
Don. 22/12/49—12/1/50.**C/L**.
10/7—24/8/50 in store.
27/8—21/9/50 in store.

BOILERS:
1075.
1076 6/02.
6810 10/06.
7336 5/8/16.
D1906 *(new)* 29/7/27.
7628 10/3/34.
8292 27/11/37.
7860 21/7/41.
7812 24/10/47.

SHEDS:
Copley Hill.
Ardsley 27/10/30.
Darlington 29/11/30.
Barnard Castle 26/4/33.
Botanic Gardens 11/11/35.
Doncaster 25/6/37.
New England 17/7/37.
South Lynn 20/7/37.
Botanic Gardens 8/9/37.
Doncaster 8/11/37.
Grantham 6/7/38.
Immingham 28/9/42.
Doncaster 22/10/44.
Grantham 19/8/45.

RENUMBERED:
4075 12/12/24.

1 14/10/44.
2000 22/10/44.
62000 12/1/50.

CONDEMNED: 18/10/51.

4076

Doncaster 728.

To traffic 6/1897.

REPAIRS:
Don. ?/?—1/04.**G**.
Don. ?/?—7/09.**G**.
Don. ?/?—18/1/19.**G**.
Rebuilt to D3.
Don. ?/?—12/20.**G**.
Don. 4/12/22—6/1/23.**L**.
Don. 2/7—15/11/24.**G**.
Don. 27/9—31/12/26.**G**.
Don. 27/9—7/11/28.**G**.
Don. 26/4—24/5/30.**G**.
Cab sides altered.
Don. 24/9—22/10/32.**G**.
Don. 26/5/36. *Not repaired.*

BOILERS:
1076.
1078 1/04.
6957 7/09.
7439 18/1/19.
7495 12/20.
7313 24/5/30.

SHEDS:
Copley Hill.
Ardsley *by* 8/27.
Copley Hill 30/6/30.

RENUMBERED:
4076 15/11/24.

CONDEMNED: 6/6/36.
Cut up at Doncaster.

4077

Doncaster 729.

To traffic 6/1897.

REPAIRS:
Don. ?/?—10/03.**G**.
Don. ?/?—6/14.**G**.
Don. 7/10—20/11/20.**G**.
Don. 26/2—19/5/23.**G**.
Rebuilt to D3.
Don. 26/10/25—8/1/26.**G**.
Don. 14/6—31/8/27.**G**.
Don. 4/5—1/6/29.**G**.
Cab sides altered.
Don. 23/5—13/6/31.**G**.
Dar. 27/7—5/8/31.**L**.
Raven F.S.A. fitted.

Don. 4—30/12/33.**G**.
Don. 26/9—6/10/34.**L**.
Don. 23/3—6/4/35.**L**.
S.W. Cab fitted.

BOILERS:
1077.
1073 10/03.
1354 6/14.
1172 20/11/20.
7657 19/5/23.
7291 1/6/29.

SHEDS:
Grantham.
Middleton-in-Teesdale 10/7/31.
Darlington 5/10/33.
Penrith 7/1/35.
Botanic Gardens 20/7/36.

RENUMBERED:
4077 17/3/25.

CONDEMNED: 26/10/37.

4078

Doncaster 730.

To traffic 6/1897.

REPAIRS:
Don. ?/?—1/03.**G**.
Don. ?/?—10/10.**G**.
Don. ?/?—27/10/17.**G**.
Rebuilt to D3.
Don. 8/3—26/8/22.**G**.
Don. 12/3—20/6/25.**G**.
Don. 21/9—23/11/27.**G**.
Don. 15/8—26/9/31.**G**.
Cab sides altered.

BOILERS:
1078.
1457 1/03.
1343 10/10.
7370 27/10/17.
7851 20/6/25.

SHEDS:
Hatfield.
Hitchin 7/9/35.

RENUMBERED:
4078 20/6/25.

CONDEMNED: 20/12/35.

4079

Doncaster 731.

To traffic 6/1897.

REPAIRS
Don. ?/?—5/08.**G**.
Don. ?/?—4/18.**G**.
Don. 24/7—4/11/22.**G**.
Don. 12/10/25—30/1/26.**G**.
Rebuilt to D3.
Don. 5/6—27/7/28.**G**.
Don. 17/5—21/6/30.**G**.
Cab sides altered.
Don. 29/10—26/11/32.**G**.

BOILERS:
1079.
1345 5/08.
6887 4/18.
7231 30/1/26.
7660 26/11/32.

SHEDS:
Grantham.
New England *still at* 2/23.
Ardsley 11/2/26.
Colwick 18/10/27.
Darlington 22/7/33.
York 9/10/34.

RENUMBERED:
4079 17/3/25.

CONDEMNED: 29/10/37.

4080

Doncaster 732.

To traffic 6/1897.

REPAIRS:
Don. ?/?—3/04.**G**.
Don. ?/?—10/10.**G**.
Don. ?/?—6/15.**G**.
Don. ?/?—2/3/18.**G**.
Rebuilt to D3
Don. 15/11/22—19/3/23.**G**.
Don. 29/6—10/10/25.**G**.
Don. 15/10—10/12/27.**G**.
Don. 14/3—23/4/30.**G**.
Cab sides altered.
Don. 10/4—15/7/33.**G**.
Don. 21—27/7/33.**N/C**.
Don. 23/10—5/12/36.**G**.
Don. 29/11/40—18/1/41.**H**.
After collision.
Don. 12/10—5/12/41.**G**.
Don. 8/10—4/11/44.**G**.

BOILERS:
1080.
1444 3/04.
1078 10/10.
1346 6/15.
7373 2/3/18.
7870 10/10/25.
7232 23/4/30.

On those with coupling rod casing, only the first eleven Nos.400 and 1071 to 1080 did not have semi-circular hinged flap at the front end to assist oiling.

Nos.4320 and 4351 to 4360 had been built with double curves to the running plate and no casing for the coupling rod. On the front curve a step was fitted.

In March 1929 it was decided that the 3ft 3in. cab cut-out was too much either for safety or to prevent draughts, and that alteration was needed. As they went for repair, the whole class then had the cut-out reduced by 9in. and in the build-up, a hand grip was also incorporated.

By April 1933 eight D3's were working on the Stainmore line in the N.E. Area and there were continuous complaints the GN cabs did not give enough protection against the weather. In 1935 Doncaster altered the cab of four by substituting a window for the cut-out, and taking the roof back a further 8 inches. Those altered were Nos.4354 (January), 4349 (February), 4077 (April) and 4075 (June). When the first one returned, it was found that Doncaster had not done anything about the horizontal handrail on the cab side, and that it was now either too short or in the wrong place.

No.4354 did not go into Darlington works or back to Doncaster, but local fitters quickly adjusted the position of the rail.

Meanwhile, the message had got through to Doncaster in time for the next one No.4349 to be fitted with a rail of full length, which had three pillars instead of just one at each end. As No.2141, the altered cab and long handrails were retained by the engine until withdrawal on 9th November 1946.

On the other two, Nos.4077 and 4075, Doncaster fitted a new and slightly longer rail but placed it centrally on the cab. Before the other four on the Stainmore line, Nos.4313, 4347, 4348 and 4350 were due to go to Doncaster for repair and cab alteration, the D3 class had been transferred away so there were only four altered. No.4077 in the meantime was put in store for some time before it was withdrawn on 26th October 1937.

4080 continued.
8179 15/7/33.
8189 5/12/41.

SHEDS:
Hitchin.
New England 16/3/28.
Boston 9/12/32.
Immingham 12/10/33.
Botanic Gardens 6/7/35.
Colwick 22/10/35.
Copley Hill 15/10/36.
Ardsley 27/3/40.
Langwith Jct. 23/7/42.
Immingham 28/9/42.
Langwith Jct. 3/10/42.

RENUMBERED:
4080 10/10/25.
2120 8/9/46.

CONDEMNED: 8/8/47.

4301

Doncaster 745.

To traffic 10/1897.

REPAIRS:
Don. ?/?—6/13.**G**.
Don. ?/?—29/7/16.**G**.
Rebuilt to D3.
Don. 2/1—13/3/20.**G**.
Don. 8/10/24—17/1/25.**G**.
Don. 7/3—20/5/27.**G**.
Don. 25/10/29—11/1/30.**G**.
Cab sides altered.
Don. 15/6—11/10/30.**H**.
Don. 26/4—11/6/32.**G**.
Don. 11/11—24/12/36.**G**.
Don. 28/10—21/1/39.**G**.
Don. 23/8—4/10/41.**G**.
Don. 17/12/43—22/1/44.**G**.
Don. 29/1—5/2/44.**N/C**.
Don. 11/7—18/8/45.**G**.
Don. 16—22/9/45.**L**.

BOILERS:
1301.
6916 6/13.
7313 29/7/16.
7630 11/1/30.
8420 4/10/41.

SHEDS:
Bradford.
King's Cross (Hatfield) 24/2/24.
Hitchin 24/11/32.
Botanic Gardens 20/10/33.
Colwick 4/12/34.
Langwith Jct. 7/8/42.
Immingham 28/9/42.
Langwith Jct. 6/12/42.

RENUMBERED:
4301 17/1/25.
2121 8/9/46.

CONDEMNED: 8/8/47.

4302

Doncaster 746.

To traffic 10/1897.

REPAIRS:
Don. ?/?—5/04.**G**.
Don. ?/?—12/08.**G**.
Don. ?/?—25/3/16.**G**.
Rebuilt to D3.
Don. 30/8—13/11/20.**G**.
Don. 14/10/24—17/1/25.**G**.
Don. 3/1—14/4/27.**G**.
Don. 27/4—1/6/29.**G**.
Cab sides altered.
Don. 18/7—22/8/31.**G**.
Don. 2/9—14/10/33.**G**.
Don. 20/3—10/4/37.**G**.
Don. 9/10—13/11/43.**G**.
Don. 22/2/48. *Not repaired.*

BOILERS:
1302.
1307 5/04.
1310 12/08.
7309 25/3/16.
8525 22/8/31.
8453 13/11/43.

SHEDS:
Ardsley.
Colwick 18/10/27.
Leicester 18/5/34.
Colwick 24/10/35.
New England 11/4/37.
South Lynn 13/5/37.
March 30/9/37.
South Lynn 12/6/38.
March 2/9/38.
South Lynn 24/5/39.
King's Lynn 19/10/39.
South Lynn 31/10/39.
Cambridge 12/12/40.
March 20/9/42.
Cambridge 21/11/42.
South Lynn 11/8/46.

RENUMBERED:
4302 17/1/25.
2122 23/9/46.

CONDEMNED: 26/2/48.
Cut up at Doncaster.

4303

Doncaster 747.

To traffic 11/1897.

REPAIRS:
Don. ?/?—12/05.**G**.
Don. ?/?—10/08.**G**.
Don. ?/?—9/4/21.**G**.
Rebuilt to D3.
Don. 3/10—5/12/25.**G**.
Don. 17/1—24/3/28.**H**.
Don. 25/2—8/4/30.**G**.
Cab sides altered.
Front heater connection fitted.
Don. 23/1—16/4/32.**G**.
Don. 2/3—19/5/34.**G**.
Don. 19/1—6/3/37.**G**.
Don. 8/10—25/11/39.**G**.
Don. 18/7—15/8/42.**G**.
Don. 3/6—8/7/44.**G**.
Don. 29/9/46—5/9/47.**G**.
Don. 30/11/49. *Not repaired.*

BOILERS:
1303.
1077 12/05.
6885 10/08.
7626 9/4/21.
7671 8/4/30.
8576 *(exJ3 3387)* 25/11/39.
8195 15/8/42.

SHEDS:
Lincoln.
Grantham 27/7/31.
Boston 23/5/34.
Immingham 8/4/37.
Louth 8/11/42.
Immingham 24/1/43.
Lincoln 17/2/43.
Colwick 26/10/47.

RENUMBERED:
4303 5/12/25.
2123 21/7/46.

CONDEMNED: 5/12/49.
Cut up at Doncaster.

4304

Doncaster 748.

To traffic 11/1897.

REPAIRS:
Don. ?/?—10/04.**G**.
Don. ?/?—3/11.**G**.
Don. ?/?—3/2/17.**G**.
Rebuilt to D3.
Don. 13/1—13/3/20.**G**.
Don. 25/4—20/8/23.**G**.

Don. 27/5—18/8/26.**G**.
Don. 21/1—27/4/29.**G**.
Front heater connection fitted.
Don. 3/10—28/11/31.**G**.
Cab sides altered.
Don. 8/11/33—13/1/34.**G**.
Don. 9/4—12/6/37.**G**.
Don. 31/5—21/8/39.**G**.
Don. 20/10/42. *Not repaired.*

BOILERS:
1304.
1080 10/04.
1075 3/11.
7351 3/2/17.
7662 20/8/23.
7379 28/11/31.
8451 21/8/39.

SHEDS:
Louth.
Lincoln 28/4/34.
Immingham 24/11/34.
Botanic Gardens 6/7/35.
Colwick 29/10/35.
Lincoln 7/3/36.
Louth 15/6/37.

RENUMBERED:
4304 18/8/26.

CONDEMNED: 7/11/42.
Cut up at Doncaster.

4305

Doncaster 749.

To traffic 11/1897.

REPAIRS:
Don. ?/?—6/04.**G**.
Don. ?/?—5/11.**G**.
Don. ?/?—5/4/13.**G**.
Rebuilt to D3.
Don. 7/4—19/6/20.**G**.
Don. 14/3/23. *To be rebuilt to Class D2*

BOILERS:
1305.
1302 6/04.
1458 5/11.
7154 5/4/13.
7486 19/6/20.

SHED:
Colwick.

4306

Doncaster 750.

To traffic 11/1897.

REPAIRS:
Don. ?/?—11/05.**G.**
Don. ?/?—15/3/13.**G.**
Rebuilt to D3.
Don. ?/?—10/18.**G.**
Don. 17/11/20—14/5/21.**G.**
Don. 13/2—17/5/24.**G.**
Don. 14/6—1/10/26.**G.**
Don. 29/8—17/10/28.**G.**
Don. 15/11—20/12/30.**G.**
Cab sides altered.
Don. 17/6—15/7/33.**G.**
Don. 9—30/11/35.**G.**
Don. 8—17/4/37.**L.**
Tablet catcher fitted.
Don. 7/7—4/8/45.**G.**
Don. 30/11—5/12/46.**L.**
Don. 29/9—13/11/48
In store tallowed.
Don. 16/11/48. *Not repaired.*

BOILERS:
1306.
1316 11/05.
7157 15/3/13.
7440 10/18.
7155 17/5/24.
D1890 *(new)* 1/10/26.
8052 15/7/33.

SHEDS:
Colwick .
New England 18/2/37.
South Lynn 13/5/37.
March 30/9/37.
South Lynn 12/6/38.
March 19/9/38.
South Lynn 8/6/39.
King's Lynn 19/10/39.
South Lynn 9/6/40.
Cambridge 15/12/40.
March 20/9/42.
Cambridge 21/11/42.
South Lynn 30/5/46.
Cambridge 11/8/46.
South Lynn 22/6/47.

RENUMBERED:
4306 17/5/24.
2124 29/9/46.

CONDEMNED: 25/11/48.
Not in use for 429 days 1944/5.

4307

Doncaster 751.

To traffic 11/1897.

REPAIRS:
Don. ?/?—2/03.**G.**
Don. ?/?—10/10.**G.**
Don. ?/?—2/6/17.**G.**
Rebuilt to D3.
Don. 2/5—4/10/22.**G.**
Don. 19/3—30/5/25.**G.**
Don. 4/1—22/3/28.**G.**
Don. 13/5—17/7/30.**G.**
Cab sides altered.
Don. 15/9—12/11/32.**G.**
Don. 10/11/32—22/5/33.
In store.
Don. 4/4—23/5/36.**G.**
Don. 13/4—21/5/38.**G.**
Don. 21/10—20/11/40.**G.**
Don. 3—30/9/44.**G.**
Don. 26/8—10/10/47.**G.**
Don. 12/8/49. *Not repaired.*

BOILERS:
1307.
1462 2/03.
867 10/10.
7368 2/6/17.
8059 22/3/28.
8683 23/5/36.
8641 21/5/38.
8057 10/10/47.

SHEDS:
Louth.
Immingham 23/6/36.
Colwick 12/8/37.
Leicester 28/2/41.
Lincoln 29/8/43.
Colwick 12/10/47.

RENUMBERED:
4307 30/5/25.
2125 19/5/46.

CONDEMNED: 15/8/49.
Cut up at Doncaster.

4308

Doncaster 752.

To traffic 12/1897.

REPAIRS:
Don. ?/?—5/04.**G.**
Don. ?/?—11/11.**G.**
Don. ?/?—17/6/16.**G.**

Rebuilt to D3.
Don. 22/8—16/12/22.**G.**
Don. 22/7—10/10/25.**G.**
Don. 13/10—24/12/27.**G.**
Don. 23/3—20/4/29.**G.**
Front heater connection fitted.
Don. 4/4—2/5/31.**G.**
Cab sides altered.
Don. 15/7—19/8/33.**G.**

BOILERS:
1308.
1445 5/04.
1311 11/11.
7317 17/6/16.
7871 10/10/25.
7876 19/8/33.

SHEDS:
York.
New England 12/23.
Ardsley 9/2/26.
Lincoln 31/12/27.
Louth 1/5/28.
Boston 25/8/31.

RENUMBERED:
4308 10/10/25.

CONDEMNED: 3/10/35.

4309

Doncaster 753.

To traffic 12/1897.

REPAIRS
Don. ?/?—7/04.**G.**
Don. ?/?—6/09.**G.**
Don. ?/?—2/2/18.**G.**
Rebuilt to D3.
Don. 21/2—24/4/20.**G.**
Don. 30/8—15/10/21.**L.**
Don. 17/4—22/9/23.**G.**
Don. 2/2—15/4/26.**G.**
Don. 25/8—17/11/28.**G.**
Don. 27/11/31—13/2/32.**G.**
Cab sides altered.
Don. 16/11—15/12/34.**G.**
Don. 6/3—6/5/39.**G.**
Don. 3/8—2/9/44.**G.**
Don. 19/7/48. *Not repaired.*

BOILERS:
1309.
1343 7/04.
6956 6/09.
7371 2/2/18.
7488 17/11/28.
7848 15/12/34.

SHEDS:
Colwick.
Leicester 28/5/27.
Colwick 15/3/28.
Leicester 21/3/29.
Colwick 24/9/30.
Leicester 23/5/32.
Colwick 10/5/34.
Lincoln 9/8/35.
Frodingham 19/5/37.
Hitchin 22/11/38.
Boston 8/6/47.
Colwick 14/9/47.

RENUMBERED:
1309N 22/9/23.
4309 15/4/26.
2126 28/9/46.

CONDEMNED: 13/8/48.
Cut up at Doncaster.

4310

Doncaster 754.

To traffic 12/1897.

REPAIRS:
Don. ?/?—8/08.**G.**
Don. ?/?—17/3/17.**G.**
Rebuilt to D3.
Don. 6/7—30/12/22.**G.**
Don. 27/2—23/5/25.**G.**
Don. 30/11/26—25/2/27.**G.**
Don. 26/10—16/11/29.**G.**
Cab sides altered.
Don. 31/12/32—28/1/33.**G.**
Don. 6—20/4/35.**G.**
Don. 20/3—10/4/37.**G.**
Don. 28/11/42—9/1/43.**G.**
Don. 30/4/47. *Not repaired.*

BOILERS:
1310.
6881 8/08.
7356 17/3/17.
7227 30/12/22.
7808 25/2/27.
7495 20/4/35.
8181 10/4/37.

SHEDS:
Colwick.
Leicester 30/4/27.
Colwick 5/4/29.
Leicester 23/5/31.
Colwick 4/11/31.
Leicester 13/10/34.
Colwick 23/2/35.
New England 6/4/37.

WORKS CODES:- Cw - Cowlairs. Dar- Darlington. Dfu - Dunfermline shed. Don - Doncaster. Ghd - Gateshead. Gor - Gorton. Inv - Inverurie. Str - Stratford.
REPAIR CODES:- **C/H** - Casual Heavy. **C/L** - Casual Light. **G**- General. **H**- Heavy. **H/I** - Heavy Intermediate. **L** - Light. **L/I** - Light Intermediate. **N/C** - Non-Classified.

South Lynn 13/5/37.
March 30/9/37.
South Lynn.1/7/38.
March 19/9/38.
South Lynn 8/6/39.
King's Lynn 19/10/39.
South Lynn 24/11/39.
March 19/9/42.
Cambridge 21/11/42.
South Lynn 15/3/43.
King's Lynn 19/8/45.
South Lynn 7/10/45.

RENUMBERED:
4310 23/5/25.
2127 18/8/46.

CONDEMNED: 20/5/47.
Cut up at Doncaster.

4311

Doncaster 759.

To traffic 3/1898.

REPAIRS:
Don. ?/?—2/10.**G.**
Don. ?/?—21/12/18.**G.**
Rebuilt to D3.
Don. 27/6—1/10/21.**G.**
Don. 17/4—4/10/24.**G.**
Don. 13/12/26—4/3/27.**G.**
Don. 29/1—13/4/29.**G.**
Don. 1/2—7/5/32.**G.**
Cab sides altered.
Don. 3/11—18/12/37.**G.**
Don. 11/9—15/11/41.**G.**
Don. 15/10—4/11/44.**G.**
Don. 14/7/46—11/1/47.**G.**
Don. 4/12/49. *Not repaired.*

BOILERS:
1311.
6986 2/10.
7441 21/12/18.
7761 4/10/24.
7672 13/4/29.
8644 18/12/37.
7858 11/1/47.

SHEDS:
Bradford.
King's Cross 13/1/24.
Ardsley 1/1/26.
Hitchin ?/?
Retford 27/7/28.
Sheffield 14/11/29.
Retford 25/1/30.
New England 23/5/32.
Boston 10/9/32.
Langwith Jct. 8/8/42.
Immingham 4/10/42.
Langwith Jct. 6/11/42.
Boston 8/6/47.

New England 14/7/47.

RENUMBERED:
4311 4/10/24.
2128 3/11/46.

CONDEMNED: 5/12/49.
Cut up at Doncaster.

4312

Doncaster 760.

To traffic 3/1898.

REPAIRS:
Don. ?/?—5/06.**G.**
Don. ?/?—7/4/17.**G.**
Rebuilt to D3.
Don. 15/6—27/8/21.**G.**
Don. 26/5—27/9/24.**G.**
Don. 2/9—6/12/26.**G.**
Don. 6/8—28/9/29.**G.**
Cab sides altered.
Don. 13/7—1/9/34.**G.**
Don. 13/8—4/9/37.**G.**
Don. 16/9—18/10/42.**G.**
Don. 22/1/46. *Not repaired.*

BOILERS:
1312.
1306 5/06.
7355 7/4/17.
7762 27/9/24.
8295 28/9/29.
7858 4/9/37.

SHEDS:
King's Cross.
Hitchin 15/6/35.
Colwick 30/11/35.
Leicester 13/3/40.
Colwick 8/8/43.
Lincoln 29/8/43.

RENUMBERED:
4312 27/9/24.
2129 allocated.

CONDEMNED: 23/2/46.
Cut up at Doncaster.

4313

Doncaster 761.

To traffic 4/1898.

REPAIRS:
Don. ?/?—11/05.**G.**
Don. ?/?—7/08.**G.**
Don. ?/?—5/10.**G.**
Don. 5/11/20—26/3/21.**G.**
Don. 19/2—16/5/24.**G.**
Rebuilt to D3.

Don. 9/3—12/5/27.**G.**
Don. 15/6—13/7/29.**G.**
Cab sides altered.
Don. 3—31/10/31.**G.**
Don. 1—24/3/34.**G.**

BOILERS:
1313.
1349 11/05.
1074 7/08.
6993 5/10.
7670 16/5/24.
7155 13/7/29.

SHEDS:
Lincoln.
Starbeck 24/11/31.
Barnard Castle 22/3/33.
Botanic Gardens 3/10/33.

RENUMBERED:
4313 16/5/24.

CONDEMNED: 23/12/35.

4314

Doncaster 762.

To traffic 5/1898.

REPAIRS:
Don. ?/?—8/08.**G.**
Don. ?/?—4/11.**G.**
Don. ?/?—12/1/18.**G.**
Rebuilt to D3.
Don. 17/8—18/11/22.**G.**
*Not back in traffic until 10/3/23
(still GNR livery).
To Plant again 26/5/23 & back
to traffic 25/8/23 still with GNR
No.1314 on cab but tender had
L&NER 1314 with paint date
3/8/23. As L&NER 1314N and
number on cab at 7/10/24.*
Don. 11/10/24—10/1/25.**G.**
Don. 30/11/27—17/2/28.**G.**
Don. 8/3—5/4/30.**G.**
Cab sides altered.
Don. 23/4—21/5/32.**G.**
Don. 20/10—10/11/34.**G.**

BOILERS:
1314.
1356 8/08.
707 4/11.
7378 12/1/18.
8061 17/2/28.

SHEDS:
King's Cross *still* 15/8/24
Lincoln ?/?
Louth 18/8/31.

RENUMBERED:
1314N *after* 3/8/23.
4314 10/1/25.

CONDEMNED: 18/6/37.

4315

Doncaster 763.

To traffic 4/1898.

REPAIRS.
Don. ?/?—2/09.**G.**
Don. ?/?—11/12.**G.**
Don. ?/?—15/5/15.**G.**
Rebuilt to D3.
Don. 16/6—24/7/20.**G.**
Don. 1/5—4/8/23.**G.**
Don. 29/12/25—6/3/26.**G.**
Don. 6/6—19/7/28.**G.**
Don. 2/8—6/9/30.**G.**
Cab sides altered.
Don. 19/8—23/9/33.**G.**
Front heater connection fitted.
Don. 9—23/5/36.**G.**
Don. 29/5/37.**L.**
Don. 16/8—6/9/41.**G.**
Don. 5/10/43.**L.**
*Not in use for 317 days during
1944.*

BOILERS:
1315.
1314 2/09.
1651 11/12.
7296 15/5/15.
7494 24/7/20.
7493 6/3/26.
7311 19/7/28.
8682 23/5/36.

SHEDS:
Colwick.
Leicester 6/4/31.
Colwick 24/3/33.
Retford 22/9/33.
Staveley 8/6/36.
New England 16/2/37.
Melton Constable18/2/37.
King's Lynn 30/5/37.
March 18/3/38.
South Lynn 22/6/38.
March 1/9/38.
South Lynn 8/6/39.
King's Lynn 16/11/39.
South Lynn 3/3/40.
March 19/9/42.
Cambridge 21/11/42.

RENUMBERED:
4315 6/3/26.
2130 29/9/46.

CONDEMNED: 29/4/47.

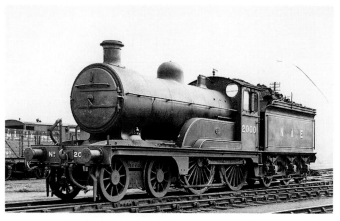

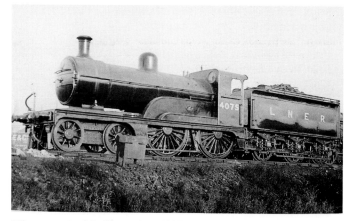

No.4075 was returned to Southern Area on 25th June 1937 and retained its altered cab until September 1944 when it underwent further change. In that month it was selected to become the engine for hauling Officer's saloon for which purpose it was re-numbered 2000, the starting number for 4-4-0 classes in the Thompson scheme.

When repaired in November 1937, No.4075 was fitted with Group Standard buffers, the only one to get that type. However, in August 1938 sister engine No.4074 changed from its original parallel shank buffers to taper shank which had been non-standard from as far back as 1905.

Steam operated sanding was fitted for forward running, the boxes being behind the frame footsteps. On the opposite side of the leading coupled wheels was gravity sanding for use in tender first running.

Until 1925 engines in the Nottingham area continued to be fitted with destination board brackets on the lower part of the smokebox. Originally the upper lamp iron was fixed on the front rim of the smokebox where two rivets indicated its position and as shown on No.1072 on page 56. When so fitted the destination board brackets were carried on the door above the top hinge. Most of the rebuilds compensated for the higher pitched boiler by having the upper lamp iron moved on to the door hence the moving of the destination board brackets to the lower position. The brackets had been removed when No.3400 was ex works 20th June 1925. It is thought that the last one to carry the brackets was No.4316 which retained them when ex works 7th March 1925.

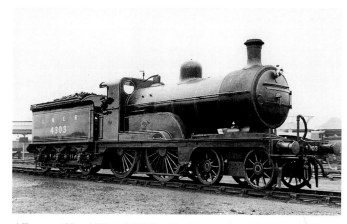

All except Nos.1071 to 1080 first had taper shank buffers with solid spindle, and at least four Nos.2115, 2125, 2135 and 2141 kept that type until withdrawal. From 1905 there was a gradual change to parallel shank type with helical springs. This parallel shank type had actually been used on the first production batch of ten engines - 1071 to 1080.

When fitted with the bigger boiler the hitherto continuous handrail was changed to end on the side of the smokebox. By Grouping all had the cross rail above the top hinge.

The cab on No.3400 differed from all the others being 5ft 2in. long and extending 6in. over the firebox casing. This cab also had a more rounded profile at the top. All the other cabs had a flat roof, were only 4ft 7in. long and did not extend over the firebox casing. Note collar on the vacuum standpipe still showing load class T as late as June 1932.

(below) Most had, and retained plain flat coupling rods but Nos.4355, 2128 and 62135 did get fluted type.

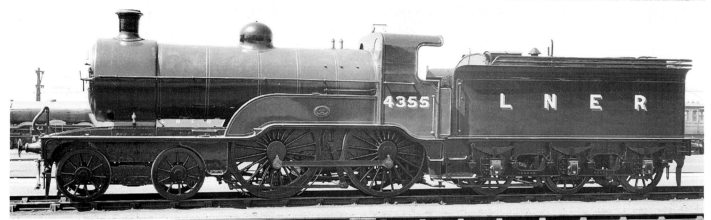

As late as May 1937 No.4306 still retained its shorter chimney acquired at rebuilding. For use on M&GN lines at least eight, Nos.3400, 4306, 4310, 4315, 4319, 4345, 4352, and 4355 were fitted with Whittaker tablet exchanging apparatus.

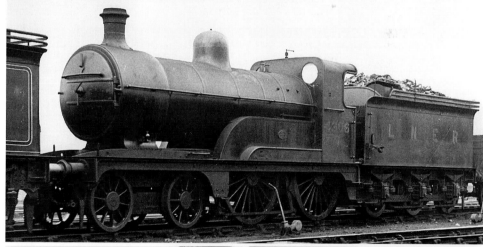

In the middle 1930's some chimneys were reduced to 2ft 5¾in. by turning 1½in. off the rim.

In 1936/7 when some began work on the M&GN and in East Anglia, J6 class chimneys 1ft 11¼in. high were fitted. From March 1939 to permit wider availability, all the others then surviving were fitted with J6 chimney.

Boilers built 1926 to 1931 had two 2½in. Ross 'Pop' safety valves mounted direct on the firebox casing but still had the vacuum ejector exhaust pipe through the boiler. However, new boilers from 1931, and any getting a new front tubeplate, then had the ejector pipe externally situated along the right hand side.

Some also had received low dome cover which cut dome height from rail level to 12ft 4⅞in. instead of 12ft 9½in.

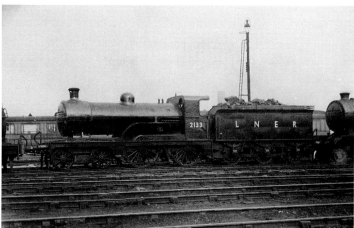

During the war, five Diagram 7 boilers were converted to Diagram 8, and these had inspection doors instead of washout plugs.

The boilers built from 1912 to 1926 had Ramsbottom safety valves in a cast iron cover.

4316

Doncaster 764.

To traffic 4/1898.

REPAIRS:
Don. ?/?—6/05.**G**.
Don. ?/?—1/12.**G**.
Don. ?/?—21/2/14.**G**.
Rebuilt to D3.
Don. ?/?—11/19.**G**.
Don. 22/2—13/7/22.G.
Don. 8/12—7/3/25.**G**.
Don. 27/1—5/4/28.**G**.
Don. 6/12/29—25/1/30.**G**.
Cab sides altered.
Don. 14/6—1/10/32.**G**.
Don. 6/10/32—4/9/33
In store.
Don. 7—22/9/33.**L**.
Front heater connection fitted.
Don. 19/5—17/7/37.**G**.
Don. 7/1—30/3/40.**G**.
Don. 18/10—19/12/42.**G**.
Don. 18/3—28/4/45.**G**.
Don. 9/2—17/3/48.**G**.

BOILERS:
   1316.
   1318 6/05.
   7080 1/12.
   7224 21/2/14.
   7157 11/19.
   7844 7/3/25.
   D1903 *(exJ3 3359)* 1/10/32.
   8454 19/12/42.

SHEDS:
Colwick.
Doncaster 21/3/25.
Mexborough 8/5/30.
Doncaster 17/5/30.
Lincoln 26/9/33.
Immingham 19/2/36.
New England 26/5/46.

RENUMBERED:
   4316 7/3/25.
   2131 8/12/46.
   62131 17/3/48.

CONDEMNED: 31/10/49.
Into Don for cut up. 2/11/49

4317

Doncaster 765.

To traffic 5/1898.

REPAIRS:
Don. ?/?—3/07.**G**.
Don. ?/?—1/2/13.**G**.
Rebuilt to D3.

Don. ?/?—12/19.**G**.
Don. 7/6—4/11/22.**G**.
Don. 8/5—25/7/25.**G**.
Don. 14/2—1/5/28.**G**.
Don. 10/7—24/8/29.**G**.
Cab sides altered.
Don. 21/10—22/12/31.**G**.
Don. 20/3—8/5/36.**G**.
Don. 16/9—23/10/37.**G**.
Don. 10/5—22/7/39.**G**.
Don. 19/6—25/7/42.**G**.
Don. 1/7—4/8/45.**G**.
Don. 7/12/47—9/1/48.**G**.

BOILERS:
1317.
1313 3/07.
7156 1/2/13.
7483 12/19.
7491 1/5/28.
8680 8/5/36.
8295 25/7/42.

SHEDS:
Colwick.
Leicester 5/9/25.
Colwick 30/4/27.
Leicester 30/5/32.
Immingham 16/10/33.
Grantham 3/11/34.
Boston 2/7/37.
Grantham 11/8/37.
Immingham 29/8/43.
Louth 17/7/49.
Boston 19/11/50.

RENUMBERED:
4317 25/7/25.
2132 1/9/46.

CONDEMNED: 7/12/50.

4318

Doncaster 766.

To traffic 5/1898.

REPAIRS:
Don. ?/?—3/05.**G**.
Don. ?/?—5/11.**G**.
Don. ?/?—4/18.**G**.
Don. ?/?—25/9/20.**G**.
Rebuilt to D3.
Don. 22/8—18/11/22.**G**.
Don. 6/6—30/7/23.**L**.
Don. 29/4—18/7/25.**G**.
Don. 8/10—23/12/27.**G**.
Don. 30/4—5/7/30.**G**.
Cab sides altered.
Don. 23/9—3/12/32.**G**.
Don. 29/5—6/7/35.**G**.
Don. 27/8—2/10/37.**G**.
Stored at Colwick from 4/11/37 to 8/12/39.

Don. 11/1—14/2/42.**G**.
Don. 29/3—29/4/44.**G**.
Don. 17/9—26/9/47.**G**.
Don. 27/8/49. *Not repaired.*

BOILERS:
1318.
1305 3/05.
7038 5/11.
7081 4/18.
7491 25/9/20.
7434 23/12/27.
7846 6/7/35.
8295 2/10/37.
8179 14/2/42.
8335 29/4/44.

SHEDS:
Colwick.
Leicester 24/10/25.
Colwick 10/4/26.
Leicester 15/3/28.
Colwick 21/3/29.
Leicester 24/3/33.
Colwick 4/10/34.
Staveley 10/8/43.
Colwick 21/10/45.
Staveley 11/11/45.
Colwick 24/3/46.
Staveley 28/9/47.

RENUMBERED:
4318 18/7/25.
2133 2/10/46.

CONDEMNED: 29/8/49.
Cut up at Doncaster.

4319

Doncaster 767.

To traffic 6/1898.

REPAIRS:
Don. ?/?—4/05.**G**.
Don. ?/?—9/10.**G**.
Don. ?/?—7/10/16.**G**.
Rebuilt to D3.
Don. 8/11/21—18/2/22.**G**.
Don. 2/1—23/2/24.**G**.
Don. 15/1—27/3/26.**G**.
Don. 30/3—6/6/28.**G**.
Don. 28/12/29—25/1/30.**G**.
Cab sides altered.
Don. 14/1—18/2/33.**G**.
Don. 15/12/34—12/1/35.**G**.
Don. 24/4—1/5/37.**L**.
Tablet catcher fitted.
Don. 7—28/10/39.**G**.
Don. 10/3—7/4/45.**G**.
Don. 28/11/46. *Not repaired.*

BOILERS:
1319.

1072 4/05.
6990 9/10.
7334 7/10/16.
7434 18/2/22.
7671 23/2/24.
7656 25/1/30.
7812 28/10/39.

SHEDS:
Leicester.
Colwick 28/5/27.
Leicester 1/4/30.
Colwick 6/4/31.
Leicester 9/5/31.
Colwick 23/5/32.
Lincoln 9/8/35.
Louth 19/10/35.
New England 15/2/37.
Melton Constable 19/2/37.
New England MGN 1/5/37.
King's Lynn 2/5/37.
March 19/3/38.
South Lynn 22/6/38.
March 1/9/38.
South Lynn 20/6/39.
Cambridge 12/12/40.
March 20/9/42.
South Lynn 1/2/43.

RENUMBERED:
4319 23/2/24.
2134 23/9/46.

CONDEMNED: 18/12/46.
Cut up at Doncaster.

4320

Doncaster 768.

To traffic 6/1898.

REPAIRS:
Don. ?/?—3/05.**G**.
Don. ?/?—4/13.**G**.
Don. ?/?—23/10/20.**G**.
Rebuilt to D3.
Don. 28/8—8/12/23.**G**.
Don. 23/4—3/5/24.**L**.
Don. 28/10/25. *To be rebuilt to Class D2*

BOILERS:
1320.
1628 3/05.
1316 4/13.
7496 23/10/20.

SHED:
Colwick.

RENUMBERED:
1320N 8/12/23.
4320 23/4/25.

(above) **At Grouping at least five, Nos.1080, 1314, 1318, 1346 as well as No.4312, are known to have had Stirling tenders, with three coal rails and a wooden buffer beam which carried the guard irons.**

(left) **The usual tender was the Ivatt Class A two coal rail type. This carried 3170 gallons of water or 3140 gallons if fitted with a scoop.**

Some had the later Class A tender with unequal axle spacing. In the 1930's Nos.4079, 4303, 4344, 4349 and 4357 definitely ran with this type.

Others had the similarly bodied early Class B type which had equal axle spacing and included a well tank giving a total water capacity of 3670 gallons.

The first post-Grouping livery had 7½in. L&NER over 12in. numbers with a small cast plate on the cab side. Three D3's were put into this style: 1080 (19/3/23), 1077 (19/5/23) and 1354 (26/5/23). By the end of June 1923 the ampersand was discarded and four got the revised LNER : 400 (7/7/23), 1318 (30/7/23), 1315 (4/8/23) and 1304 (20/8/23).

(right) From late August 1923 to the end of January 1924 the Area suffix N was added to the number and four had this applied: 1348N (24/8/23), 1309N (22/9/23), 1352N (17/11/23) and 1349N (12/1/24).

(below) Beginning with No.4319 ex works 23rd February 1924, all the others went straight to 1924 numbering.

4341

Doncaster 802.

To traffic 12/1898.

REPAIRS:
Don. ?/?—4/09.**G.**
Don. ?/?—14/8/15.**G.**
Rebuilt to D3
Don. 23/3—8/6/18.**G.**
Don. 17/11/23—8/3/24.**G.**
Don. 3—26/7/24.**L.**
Don. 6/6—27/8/27.**G.**
Don. 12/7—16/8/30.**G.**
Cab sides altered.
Don. 4—25/6/32.**G.**

BOILERS:
1341.
1348 4/09.
7290 14/8/15.
7154 8/3/24.
7870 16/8/30.

SHEDS:
Doncaster.
Leicester 4/8/33.
Botanic Gardens 4/10/33.
Colwick 4/12/34.

RENUMBERED:
4341 8/3/24.

CONDEMNED: 9/7/37.

4342

Doncaster 803.

To traffic 11/1898.

REPAIRS:
Don. ?/?—6/12.**G.**
Don. ?/?—24/11/17.**G.**
Rebuilt to D3.
Don. 14/2—27/5/22.**G.**
Don. 10/8—24/10/25.**G.**
Don. 22/12/27—8/3/28.**G.**
Don. 26/9—24/10/31.**G.**
Cab sides altered.
Don. 24/3—14/4/34.**G.**

BOILERS:
1342.
7081 6/12.
7366 24/11/17.
8060 8/3/28.
8293 14/4/34.

SHEDS:
Doncaster *still in* 1926.
New England ?/?
Retford 19/3/32.
Copley Hill 29/6/36.

RENUMBERED:
4342 24/10/25.

CONDEMNED: 14/11/36.

4343

Doncaster 804.

To traffic 12/1898.

REPAIRS:
Don. ?/?—5/04.**G.**
Don. ?/?—2/11.**G.**
Don. ?/?—21/4/17.**G.**
Rebuilt to D3.
Don. 1/11/20—5/3/21.**G.**
Don. 9/10/24—10/1/25.**G.**
Don. 27/8—3/11/27.**G.**
Don. 24/2—5/4/30.**G.**
Cab sides altered.
Don. 29/3—24/6/33.**G.**
Don. 27/11/35—11/1/36.**G.**
Don. 30/4—18/6/38.**G.**
Don. 13/2—10/3/42.**G.**
Don. 9/9—13/10/45.**G.**
Don. 10/5—15/6/48.**G.**

BOILERS:
1343.
1458 5/04.
1320 2/11.
7357 21/4/17.
7841 10/1/25.
7634 24/6/33.
7808 11/1/36.
8730 13/10/45.

SHEDS:
Boston.
New England 2/2/28.
Boston 10/12/32.
Louth 13/10/33.
Lincoln 28/9/38.
Colwick 26/10/47.

RENUMBERED:
4343 10/1/25.
2135 2/6/46.
62135 15/6/48.

CONDEMNED: 6/2/50.
Into Don. for cut up 8/2/50.

4344

Doncaster 805.

To traffic 12/1898.

REPAIRS:
Don. ?/?—8/06.**G.**
Don. ?/?—12/08.**G.**
Don. ?/?—6/15.**G.**
Don. ?/?—8/12/17.**G.**
Rebuilt to D3.
Don. 17/8/21—21/1/22.**G.**
Don. 27/6—18/10/24.**G.**
Don. 4/4—18/6/27.**G.**
Don. 29/4—29/6/29.**G.**
Cab sides altered.
Don. 8/5—8/8/31.**G.**
Don. 21/2—7/4/34.**G.**
Don. 22/9—23/10/37.**G.**
Don. 4/1—18/2/43.**G.**
Don. 26/7—1/9/45.**G.**
Don. 22/10/47. *Not repaired.*

BOILERS:
1344.
1355 8/06.
6914 12/08.
1652 6/15.
7364 8/12/17.
7813 18/6/27.
7846 23/10/37.

SHEDS:
Retford.
Sheffield 31/8/25.
Grantham 20/12/25.
Boston 6/4/34.
New England 6/5/34.
Boston 26/5/37.
Immingham 28/9/42.
Boston 18/8/46.
Colwick 14/9/47.

RENUMBERED:
4344 18/10/24.
2136 29/9/46.

CONDEMNED: 28/11/47.
Cut up at Doncaster.

4345

Doncaster 806.

To traffic 12/1898.

REPAIRS:
Don. ?/?—10/05.**G.**
Don. ?/?—2/11.**G.**
Don. ?/?—24/2/17.**G.**
Rebuilt to D3.
Don. 23/11/18—15/2/19.**G.**
Don. 8/12/23—29/3/24.**G.**
Don. 13/9—24/12/26.**G.**
Don. 23/11—31/12/29.**G.**
Cab sides altered.
Don. 26/3—23/4/32.**G.**
Don. 12/5—9/6/34.**L.**
Don. 2—30/11/35.**G.**
Don. 19/6—10/7/37.**G.**
Don. 14/10—25/11/39.**G.**
Don. 30/1—27//2/43.**G.**
Don. 27/2—29/3/47.**G.**
Don. 4/1/49. *Not repaired.*

BOILERS:
1345.
1357 10/05.
1074 2/11.
7360 24/2/17.
7667 29/3/24.
7631 31/12/29.
D1899 *(ex4356)* 30/11/35.
8180 29/3/47.

SHEDS:
Doncaster.
Mexborough 5/5/30.
Doncaster 19/5/30.
Leicester 4/8/33.
Botanic Gardens 4/10/33.
Colwick 4/12/34.
New England 18/2/37.
Melton Constable 1/3/37.
Norwich 26/11/39.
Melton Constable 18/12/39.
Yarmouth Beach 29/7/41.
Melton Constable 31/8/41.
Norwich 18/12/41.
Melton Constable 23/4/42.
Norwich 8/5/42.
Yarmouth Beach 18/6/42.
South Lynn 26/7/43.
Cambridge 21/8/45.
South Lynn 22/6/47.

RENUMBERED:
4345 29/3/24.
2137 18/8/46.

CONDEMNED: 8/1/49.
Cut up at Doncaster.

4346

Doncaster 807.

To traffic 12/1898.

REPAIRS:
Don. ?/?—12/08.**G.**
Don. ?/?—4/13.**G.**
Don. ?/?—8/12/17.**G.**
Rebuilt to D3.
Don. ?/?—6/20.**G.**
Don. 30/9—16/12/22.**G.**
Don. 19/11—21/2/25.**G.**
Don. 23/8—26/11/26.**H.**
Don. 30/1—1/6/28.**G.**
Don. 23/12/32—18/2/33.**G.**
Cab sides altered.
Don. 7/7—21/8/37.**G.**
Don. 4—26/8/40.**G.**
Don. 23/11—18/12/43.**G.**
In store 25/2 to 6/10/33
& 3/12/35 to 2/3/37.

BOILERS:
1346.
6916 12/08.

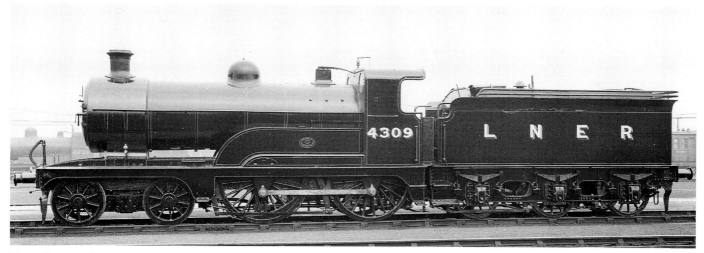

From June 1929 the number was put on the cab side in 9in. figures and LNER on the tender became 12in. The small number plate hitherto on the cab disappeared but single red lining was retained until 1941.

Only two of the class acquired their full BR numbers on black unlined paint. They were 62131 (17/3/48) and 62135 (15/6/48) Both figures and letters were 10in. deep but the 6 was of the modified type. The sole engine to acquire a smokebox number plate was 62135. No.62131 was the only member of the class to have separate splashers, which were retained to withdrawal.

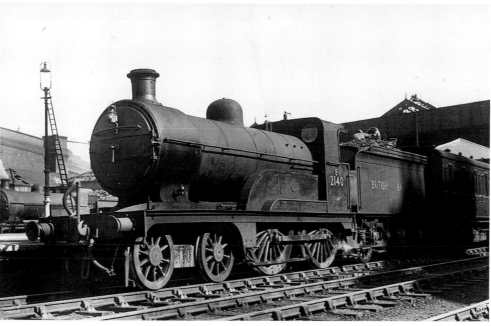

After the change to 1946 numbers and the restoration of LNER from the wartime NE, the supply of transfers began to dry up and yellow painted unshaded numbers began to appear from April 1947 in Gill sans style, figures were 9in. high whilst LNER was still 12in. Previous 'home-grown' renumbering at sheds in 1946 had produced hand painted and even stencilled examples which were not of the best quality. Seven D3's got the official painted 9in. Gill sans numbers: 2123 (5/9/47), 2125 (10/10/47), 2132 (9/1/48), 2133 (26/9/47), 2139 (19/9/47), 2145 (20/12/47), 2148 (25/5/47). Out 9th March 1948, No.2140 had the E prefix over its number which was now 12in. against the 10in. of BRITISH RAILWAYS on the tender.

4346 continued.
1319 4/13.
7380 8/12/17.
7493 6/20.
7634 16/12/22.
7844 18/2/33.
8177 26/8/40.

SHEDS:
King's Cross.
Hitchin 25/2/33.
Botanic Gardens 26/10/33.
Hitchin 4/12/34.
Colwick 4/12/35.
Leicester 26/9/37.
Colwick 18/2/40.
Leicester 2/7/41.
Colwick 22/8/41.
Boston 1/9/43.
Immingham 14/2/45.

RENUMBERED:
4346 21/2/25.
2138 29/9/46.

CONDEMNED: 8/8/47.

4347

Doncaster 808.

To traffic 12/1898.

REPAIRS:
Don. ?/?—6/04.**G.**
Don. ?/?—6/09.**G.**
Don. ?/?—11/7/14.**G.**
Rebuilt to D3.
Don. 29/1—8/3/19.**G.**
Don. 10—17/10/19.**L.**
Don. 26/6—29/11/24.**G.**
Don. 26/1—4/4/25.**H.**
Don. 21/7—30/10/28.**G.**
Don. 9/2—25/4/31.**G.**
Cab sides altered.
Dar. 13—19/5/31.**L.**
Raven F.S.A. fitted.
Dar. 22/3—5/5/33.**L.**
Don. 30/9—28/10/33.**G.**
Don. 5/5—30/6/36.**G.**
Don. 23/10—6/11/37.**L.**
Don. 8/10—2/12/39.**G.**
Don. 29/7—15/8/42.**G.**
Don. 23/5—24/6/44.**G.**
Don. 15/8—19/9/47.**G.**

BOILERS:
1347.
867 6/04.
1077 6/09.
7225 11/7/14.
7308 29/11/24.
7492 25/4/31.
8645 30/6/36.
8644 19/9/47.

SHEDS:
Doncaster.
Mexborough.
Woodford Halse 14/6/29.
Mexborough 4/7/29.
Doncaster 10/7/29.
Darlington 5/3/31.
Barnard Castle 5/10/33.
Selby 13/11/35.
Doncaster 24/6/37.
New England 15/7/37.
South Lynn 17/7/37.
Botanic Gardens 8/9/37.
Doncaster 8/11/37.
Lincoln 16/12/37.
Immingham 17/7/39.
Langwith Jct. 21/11/42.
Immingham 29/11/42.
Louth 28/3/48.

RENUMBERED:
4347 29/11/24.
2139 29/11/46.

CONDEMNED: 13/6/49.
Into Don. for cut up 15/6/49.

4348

Doncaster 809.

To traffic 12/1898.

REPAIRS:
Don. ?/?—9/08.**G.**
Don. ?/?—1/5/15.**G.**
Rebuilt to D3.
Don. 20/5—8/10/21.**G.**
Don. 9/5—24/8/23.**G.**
Don. 3/9/26—5/1/27.**G.**
Don. 7/5—6/8/27.**G.**
After collision.
Don. 30/8—5/10/29.**G.**
Cab sides altered.
Dar. 18—28/10/30.**N/C.**
Raven F.S.A. fitted.
Dar. 9—12/6/31.**N/C.**
Don. 28/11/31—9/1/32.**G.**
Don. 23/12/33—27/1/34.**G.**
Don. 30/10—20/11/37.**G.**
Don. 28/11/40—18/1/41.**L.**
Don. 26/12/42—23/1/43.**G.**
Don. 8/7—18/8/45.**G.**
Don. 6/2—9/3/48.**G.**
In store 5/2/39 to 8/3/40.

BOILERS:
1348.
6880 9/08.
7299 1/5/15.
7630 8/10/21.
8293 5/10/29.
D1890 (*ex4306*) 27/1/34.
8648 9/3/48.

SHEDS:
Doncaster.
York 12/23.
Darlington 23/9/30.
York 6/11/30.
Darlington 27/11/30.
Botanic Gardens 21/7/36.
Doncaster 8/11/37.
Lincoln 9/12/37.
New England 27/7/38.
Lincoln 27/9/38.
Immingham 8/3/40.
Retford 10/3/46.
Colwick 11/8/47.
Staveley 19/3/50.
Colwick 23/4/50.

RENUMBERED:
1348N 24/8/23.
4348 24/4/25.
2140 29/9/46.
E**2140** 9/3/48.

CONDEMNED: 15/6/50.

4349

Doncaster 810.

To traffic 12/1898.

REPAIRS:
Don. ?/?—9/05.**G.**
Don. ?/?—6/09.**G.**
Don. ?/?—2/10/15.**G.**
Rebuilt to D3.
Don. 9/3—18/5/18.**G.**
Don. 1/10/23—12/1/24.**G.**
Don. 22/6—3/10/25.**G.**
Don. 13/9—10/12/26.**H.**
Don. 24/12/28—2/3/29.**G.**
Don. 8/9—1/11/30.**G.**
Cab sides altered.
Dar. 23/4—8/5/31.**L.**
Raven F.S.A. fitted.
Dar. 18—23/6/31.**N/C.**
Don. 22/4—8/7/33.**G.**
Don. 21/1—16/2/35.**H.**
Cab to Dwg. Y1391N.
Don. 23/10—13/11/37.**G.**
Don. 19/2—28/3/42.**G.**
Don. 7/7—12/8/44.**G.**
Don. 5/3—24/3/45.
Special Exam.
Don. 27/12/45—12/1/46.**L.**
Don. 16/9/46. *Not repaired.*

BOILERS:
1349.
1308 9/05.
6955 6/09.
7298 2/10/15.
7665 12/1/24.
7365 2/3/29.
8060 16/2/35.

SHEDS:
Doncaster.
Darlington 5/1/31.
Barnard Castle 24/8/33.
Kirkby Stephen 5/10/33.
Botanic Gardens 11/11/35.
Doncaster 25/6/37.
New England 17/7/37.
Boston 21/7/37.
Botanic Gardens 8/10/37.
Doncaster 8/11/37.
Lincoln 3/3/38.
New England 27/7/38.
Grantham 25/4/40.
Immingham 20/8/43.

RENUMBERED:
1349N 12/1/24.
4349 3/10/25.
2141 6/10/46.

CONDEMNED: 9/11/46.
Cut up at Doncaster.

4350

Doncaster 811.

To traffic 12/1898.

REPAIRS:
Don. ?/?—5/05.**G.**
Don. ?/?—5/10.**G.**
Don. ?/?—27/5/16.**G.**
Rebuilt to D3.
Don. 26/10/21—25/2/22.**G.**
Don. 30/10/24—27/2/25.**G.**
Don. 22/10/27—21/1/28.**G.**
Don. 9/4—11/7/31.**G.**
Cab sides altered.
Dar. 22/9—7/10/31.**L.**
Raven F.S.A. fitted.
Dar. 6—17/11/31.**N/C.**
Don. 23/12/33—27/1/34.**G.**
Don. 8—22/11/37.**G.**
Don. 20/2—3/5/42.**G.**
Don. 28/7—26/8/44.**G.**
Don. 16/3/47. *Not repaired.*
In store 19/12/37 to 23/1/39
& 21/5/39 to 8/3/40.

BOILERS:
1350.
1320 5/05.
6985 5/10.
7320 27/5/16.
8055 21/1/28.
8057 22/11/37.

SHEDS:
Boston.
Darlington 14/7/31.
Botanic Gardens 29/6/34.
Doncaster 8/11/37.

Lincoln 4/3/38.
Immingham 8/3/40.

RENUMBERED:
4350 27/2/25.
2142 6/10/46.

CONDEMNED: 29/4/47.
Cut up at Doncaster.

4351

Doncaster 862.

To traffic 11/1899.

REPAIRS:
Don. ?/?—1/06.**G.**
Don. ?/?—6/07.**G.**
Don. ?/?—11/11.**G.**
Don. ?/?—21/9/18.**G.**
Rebuilt to D3.
Don. 3/3—7/5/21.**G.**
Don. 18/7—1/11/24.**G.**
Don. 27/8—11/11/27.**G.**
Don. 18/10—20/12/30.**G.**
Cab sides altered.
Don. 17/4—15/7/33.**G.**
Don. 27/9—31/10/36.**G.**
Don. 1/11—4/12/37.**L.**
Tender changed due to collision.
Don. 1/12/41—17/1/42.**G.**
Don. 1—21/10/44.**G.**
Don. 22/2—10/3/45.**L.**
Don. 1/3/48. *Not repaired.*

BOILERS:
1351.
1345 1/06.
1352 6/07.
7032 11/11.
7431 21/9/18.
7356 11/11/27.
7857 15/7/33.
D1893 *(ex4074)* 31/10/36.

SHEDS:
York.
Boston 16/1/25.
New England 29/12/36.
Grantham 24/10/42.
New England 4/6/43.
Louth 24/8/43.
Immingham 16/3/47.
Louth 4/5/47.

RENUMBERED:
4351 1/11/24.
2143 20/10/46.

CONDEMNED: 23/3/48.
Cut up at Doncaster.

4352

Doncaster 863.

To traffic 11/1899.

REPAIRS:
Don. ?/?—5/06.**G.**
Don. ?/?—1/10.**G.**
Don. ?/?—11/7/14.**G.**
Rebuilt to D3.
Don. 1/11/21—21/2/22.**G.**
Don. 19/9—17/11/23.**G.**
Don. 22/1—3/4/26.**G.**
Don. 28/2—4/5/28.**G.**
Don. 2—30/8/30.**G.**
Cab sides altered.
Don. 25/2—25/3/33.**G.**
Don. 23/2—16/3/35.**G.**
Don. 8—17/4/37.**L.**
Tablet catcher fitted.
Don. 24/1—21/2/42.**G.**
Don. 20/5—5/6/44.**L.**
Don. 27/2—22/3/47.**G.**
Don. 20/7/48. *Not repaired.*

BOILERS:
1352.
1354 5/06.
6963 1/10.
7227 11/7/14.
7367 21/2/22.
7664 17/11/23.
7495 30/8/30.
7666 16/3/35.
8180 21/2/42.
7654 22/3/47.

SHEDS:
Leicester.
Colwick 5/9/25.
Leicester 5/4/29.
Colwick 9/10/29.
New England 23/2/37.
South Lynn 26/7/37.
March 19/9/38.
South Lynn 20/6/39.
March 19/9/42.
South Lynn 20/7/43.

RENUMBERED:
1352N 17/11/23.
4352 3/4/26.
2144 27/10/46.

CONDEMNED: 3/8/48.
Cut up at Doncaster.

4353

Doncaster 864.

To traffic 11/1899.

REPAIRS:
Don. ?/?—12/07.**G.**
Don. ?/?—4/08.**G.**
Don. ?/?—3/11.**G.**
Don. ?/?—28/4/17.**G.**
Rebuilt to D3.
Don. 12/4—1/10/21.**G.**
Don. 13/2—11/6/24.**G.**
Don. 14/9—4/12/26.**G.**
Don. 2/2—9/3/29.**G.**
Don. 25/7—29/8/31.**G.**
Cab sides altered.
Don. 28/10—2/12/33.**G.**

BOILERS:
1353.
1345 12/07.
1351 4/08.
7039 3/11.
7367 28/4/17.
7629 1/10/21.
7319 4/12/26.
8526 29/8/31.

SHED:
Colwick.

RENUMBERED:
4353 11/6/24.

CONDEMNED: 30/4/36.

4354

Doncaster 865.

To traffic 12/1899.

REPAIRS:
Don. ?/?—11/05.**G.**
Don. ?/?—1/3/13.**G.**
Rebuilt to D3.
Don. ?/?—5/20.**G.**
Don. 12/2—26/5/23.**G.**
Don. 8—28/8/24.**H.**
Don. 19/10/25—8/1/26.**G.**
Don. 28/2—2/6/28.**G.**
Don. 31/5—12/7/30.**G.**
Cab sides altered.
Dar. 9—24/12/30.**L.**
Raven F.S.A. fitted.
Dar. 9—26/1/31.**N/C.**
Dar. 24—26/6/31.**N/C.**
Don. 18/3—15/4/33.**G.**
Don. 11/8—1/9/34.**G.**
Don. 12—19/1/35.**L.**

Cab altered.
Dar. 28/6/35. *Weigh.*

BOILERS:
1354.
1319 11/05.
7159 1/3/13.
7488 5/20.
7431 2/6/28.
8644 1/9/34.

SHEDS:
Colwick.
Ardsley 10/7/30.
Copley Hill 15/7/30.
Ardsley 27/10/30.
Darlington 15/11/30.
Middleton-in-Teesdale 5/10/33.
Botanic Gardens 14/7/36.

RENUMBERED:
4354 28/8/24.

CONDEMNED: 29/10/37.

4355

Doncaster 866.

To traffic 12/1899.

REPAIRS:
Don. ?/?—12/05.**G.**
Don. ?/?—11/11.**G.**
Don. ?/?—12/8/16.**G.**
Rebuilt to D3.
Don. 5/7—8/10/21.**G.**
Don. 2/1—15/3/24.**G.**
Don. 7/4—24/7/26.**G.**
Don. 13/11—29/12/28.**G.**
Don. 29/8—3/10/31.**G.**
Cab sides altered.
Don. 4/11—2/12/33.**G.**
Don. 3—17/10/36.**G.**
Don. 30/3—3/4/37.**L.**
Tablet catcher fitted.
Don. 29/4—10/6/39.**G.**
Don. 15/8—5/9/42.**G.**
Don. 6/5—3/6/44.**G.**
Don. 24/11—20/12/47.**G.**
Don. 2—10/3/48.**L.**
Don. 4/1/49. *Not repaired.*

BOILERS:
1355.
1652 12/05.
7036 11/11.
7316 12/8/16.
7632 8/10/21.
7672 15/3/24.
7302 29/12/28.
7807 3/10/31.

WORKS CODES:- Cw - Cowlairs. Dar- Darlington. Dfu - Dunfermline shed. Don - Doncaster. Ghd - Gateshead. Gor - Gorton. Inv - Inverurie. Str - Stratford.
REPAIR CODES:- **C/H** - Casual Heavy. **C/L** - Casual Light. **G** - General. **H** - Heavy. **H/I** - Heavy Intermediate. **L** - Light. **L/I** - Light Intermediate. **N/C** - Non-Classified.

73

4355 continued.
8649 17/10/36.
8527 20/12/47.

SHEDS:
Colwick.
Leicester 8/10/29.
Colwick 1/4/30.
Leicester 23/2/35.
Colwick 12/5/36.
New England 18/2/37.
New England MGN 24/4/37.
Melton Constable 1/5/37.
Yarmouth Beach 8/3/40.
Norwich 24/12/41.
Melton Constable 2/2/42.
Norwich 10/5/42.
Melton Constable 17/1/43.
Norwich 4/7/43.
South Lynn 16/7/43.

RENUMBERED:
4355 15/3/24.
2145 3/11/46.
E2145 10/3/48.

CONDEMNED: 8/1/49.
Cut up at Doncaster.

4356

Doncaster 867.

To traffic 12/1899.

REPAIRS:
Don. ?/?—11/07.**G**.
Don. ?/?—5/09.**G**.
Don. ?/?—4/11.**G**.
Don. 22/9—3/12/21.**G**.
Don. 15/9—5/12/24.**G**.
Don. 8/6—28/9/27.**G**.
Rebuilt to D3.
Don. 11/1—8/2/30.**G**.
Cab sides altered.
Don. 18/6—16/7/32.**G**.
Don. 23/2—16/3/35.**G**.
Don. 3—24/4/37.**G**.
Don. 2—23/10/43.**G**.
Don. 1/6/46. *Not repaired.*

BOILERS:
1356.
1317 11/07.
1346 5/09.
7041 4/11.
D1899 *(new)* 28/9/27.
D1906 *(ex4075)* 16/3/35.

SHEDS:
Boston.
Grantham 14/3/36.
New England 26/4/37.
South Lynn 26/7/37.

March 1/10/37.
South Lynn 29/6/38.
March 29/1/39.
South Lynn 20/6/39.
King's Lynn 19/10/39.
South Lynn 31/10/39.
Cambridge 12/12/40.
March 20/9/42.
South Lynn 26/7/43.

RENUMBERED:
4356 5/12/24.
2146 allocated.

CONDEMNED: 15/6/46.
Cut up at Doncaster.

4357

Doncaster 868.

To traffic 12/1899.

REPAIRS:
Don. ?/?—6/05.**G**.
Don. ?/?—2/9/16.**G**.
Rebuilt to D3.
Don. 19/10—20/11/20.**G**.
Don. 21/9—12/12/25.**G**.
Don. 15/5—25/7/28.**G**.
Don. 30/12/30—14/3/31.**G**.
Cab sides altered.
Don. 9/9—4/11/33.**G**.
Don. 6/1—7/3/36.**G**.
Don. 23/3—7/5/38.**G**.
Don. 21/11—21/12/40.**G**.
Don. 18/10—20/11/43.**G**.
Don. 7/6/47. *Not repaired.*

BOILERS:
1357.
1347 6/05.
7339 2/9/16.
7499 20/11/20.
7377 14/3/31.
7356 4/11/33.
8641 7/3/36.
8055 7/5/38.

SHEDS:
Boston.
Immingham 16/4/45.

RENUMBERED:
4357 12/12/25.
2147 17/2/46.

CONDEMNED: 19/6/47.
Cut up at Doncaster.

4358

Doncaster 869.

To traffic 12/1899.

REPAIRS:
Don. ?/?—3/07.**G**.
Don. ?/?—7/12.**G**.
Don. 23/5—14/10/22.**G**.
Don. 4/6—1/9/25.**G**.
Don. 10/4—30/6/28.**G**.
Rebuilt to D3.
Don. 12/7—16/8/30.**G**.
Cab sides altered.
Don. 25/2—25/3/33.**G**.
Don. 1—22/6/35.**G**.

BOILERS:
1358.
1359 3/07.
7083 7/12.
7351 30/6/28.
D1901 *(exJ3 4036)* 22/6/35.

SHED:
Boston.

RENUMBERED:
4358 1/9/25.

CONDEMNED: 14/8/37.

4359

Doncaster 870.

To traffic 12/1899.

REPAIRS:
Don. ?/?—12/05.**G**.
Don. ?/?—9/11/12.**G**.
Rebuilt to D3.
Don. 10/1—29/7/22.**G**.
Don. 13/10/24—17/1/25.**G**.
Don. 27/8—22/11/27.**G**.
Don. 4/10—6/1/30.**G**.
Cab sides altered.
Don. 11/11/33—20/1/34.**G**.
Don. 31/8—2/10/37.**G**.
Don. 1/3—25/4/42.**G**.
Don. 20/4—25/5/47.**G**.

BOILERS:
1359.
1651 12/05.
7153 9/11/12.
7354 29/7/22.
7842 17/1/25.
7375 22/11/27.
8061 2/10/37.
8292 25/4/42.

SHEDS:
Boston.
Hitchin 2/1/44.
Colwick 8/5/49.
Staveley 4/9/49.
Colwick 18/9/49.

RENUMBERED:
4359 17/1/25.
2148 27/7/46.

CONDEMNED: 20/11/50.
Into Don. for cut up 21/11/50.

4360

Doncaster 871.

To traffic 12/1899.

REPAIRS:
Don. ?/?—7/08.**G**.
Don. ?/?—3/10.**G**.
Don. ?/?—4/18.**G**.
Don. 26/4—13/8/21.**G**.
Don. 16/9—20/12/24.**G**.
Don. 18/6—30/9/27.**G**.
Rebuilt to D3.
Don. 12/4—10/5/30.**G**.
Cab sides altered.
Don. 17/12/32—7/1/33.**G**.

BOILERS:
1360.
1353 7/08.
6988 3/10.
6881 4/18.
D1910 *(new)* 30/9/27.

SHED:
Boston.

RENUMBERED:
4360 20/12/24.

CONDEMNED: 25/10/35.

The official photograph of No.2000 after its special treatment in 1944 in readiness for hauling officer's saloons and special trains. As can be seen it got a cab with two side windows, hinged glass sight screens, brass cap to chimney, green fully lined livery with hand painted coat-of-arms. But it lost Group Standard buffers and had its original GNR type fitted. The boiler which was 19½ years old still had Ramsbottom safety valves. In October 1947 the number and NE on the tender in shaded transfers were superseded by yellow painted unshaded Gill sans with LNER restored. The boiler was changed to one with Ross 'Pops' but that replacement had started work in January 1927. It did however have a tender of the later Class B built in June 1920.

From a light repair on 12th January 1950, it came out with BR number which had the correct Gill sans 6 on the smokebox plate but the modified variety on the cab side. The tender had LNER and crest painted over (not very effectively) and the small BR emblem put on, the LNER green being retained.

4316 had been at Colwick but on 21st March went to Doncaster shed who loaned it to Mexborough from 8th to 17th May 1930. It moved from Doncaster to Lincoln on 26th September 1933, after being stored from 6th October 1932 to 4th September 1933. Whilst at Lincoln it worked, amongst other trains, these empty iron ore hoppers for High Dyke sidings and is seen between Grantham and Great Ponton.

(above) Despite earlier variations, the five which the LNER took over were all alike in details. The Midland pattern tender holding 3 tons of coal and 3000 gallons of water, had superseded the original smaller tender at the second rebuilding.

(left) All five had Whittaker type tablet exchanging apparatus fitted on the tender. They also had a raised brass figure on the upper side sheet of the cab to indicate their power classification. Because LNER classification for the exM&GN engines was only introduced in July 1942, they remained 'A Rebuild' as the last one was withdrawn 23rd May 1941.

M&GN Class A - No LNER classification.

(0)23

Beyer, Peacock 2107.

To traffic 1881.

REPAIRS:
MC. ?/?—?/11/19.**G.** *Rebuilt.*
Str. *by* 19/12/36.
Not repaired.

BOILER:
23.

SHED:
New England (M&GN)
at 1/10/36.

CONDEMNED: 6/2/37.
Cut up at Stratford.

025

Beyer, Peacock 2338.

To traffic 11/1883.

REPAIRS:
MC. ?/?—?/6/20.**G.** *Rebuilt.*
MC. ?/?—12/11/36.**G.**
Str. 7/1—16/6/37.**H.**
Str. 29/11—29/12/39.**G.**
Str. 12/3/41. *Not repaired.*
Cracked frame.

BOILER:
25.

SHED:
New England (M&GN)
at 1/10/36.

RENUMBERED:
025 12/11/36.

CONDEMNED: 23/5/41.
Cut up at Stratford.

(0)26

Beyer, Peacock 2339.

To traffic 1883.

REPAIRS:
MC. ?/?—?/5/23.**G.** *Rebuilt.*
Str. 10/10/36. *Not repaired.*

BOILER:
26.

SHED:
Peterborough East *at* 1/10/36.

CONDEMNED: 4/11/36.
Cut up at Stratford.

027

Beyer, Peacock 2340.

To traffic 1883.

REPAIRS:
MC. ?/?—?/3/27.**G.** *Rebuilt.*
Str. *by* 19/12/36. *Not repaired.*

BOILER:
27.

SHED:
South Lynn *at* 1/10/36.

RENUMBERED:
027 ?/11/36.

CONDEMNED: 3/2/37.
Cut up at Stratford.

(0)28

Beyer, Peacock 2341.

To traffic 1883.

REPAIRS:
MC. ?/?—?/2/25.**G.** *Rebuilt.*

BOILER:
28.

SHEDS:
New England (M&GN)
at 1/10/36.

CONDEMNED: 16/2/38.
Cut up at Stratford.

(opposite, bottom) **In November 1936, Melton Constable changed No.25 to 025 but after reaching Stratford on the 7th January 1937 it was given a heavy repair, being ex works on the 16th June 1937 in unlined black with 025 and LNER in normal 12in. transfers with shading. As shown, it kept the combined steam and vacuum brake valve, in which the small ejector was expected to act as a blower. Note the Midland power class 1 was undisturbed.**

(left) **Of the five which reached LNER, only two got evidence of that ownership. In November 1936 Melton Constable removed the brass numerals from No.27 and put hand painted, unshaded 027 on the cab, but left M&GN on the tender. As such it got to Stratford by 19th December 1936 only to be withdrawn on 3rd February 1937. Nos.23, 26 and 28 retained their brass numbers being withdrawn on 6th February 1937, 4th November 1936 and 16th February 1938 respectively.**

The LNER found the blower arrangement unsatisfactory and soon put on a separate blower with the control rod along the right hand side of the boiler.

No.025 on one of its three visits to Stratford works.

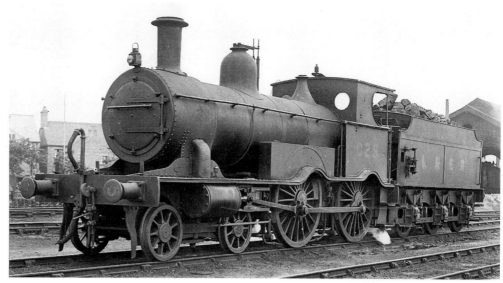

025's allocation was the M&GN road at New England shed but it was usually sub-shedded at Spalding as here in 1938. Occasionally it was used on the single daily through train from Spalding to Nottingham (Midland) but mainly worked local passenger and goods trains no further west than Bourne and to South Lynn eastward. Its 23rd May 1941 withdrawal made Class A extinct.

No.26 had an exceedingly brief LNER existence. Taken over 1st October 1936, it arrived at Stratford works on the 10th October, no repair was done and on 4th November 1936 it was withdrawn. It was allocated to Peterborough East shed and here, on a goods to South Lynn, is crossing Sutton bridge.

No.28, allocated to Peterborough was latterly sub-shedded at Bourne and here in July 1937 is at Edmondthorpe & Wymondham on the 8.15 a.m. school train to Saxby. It remained in M&GN style until withdrawn.

Beyer, Peacock built seven more in 1899 and of these, six Nos.74, 75, 76, 78, 79 and 80 remained at take-over with only detail alterations.

From about 1907, extended smokebox had been fitted, but the Johnson pattern of smokebox door with a plate hinge was retained as was the continuous handrail.

By 1931, when No.3 was changed, all the Johnson doors had been superseded by the later Midland design which had hinge straps and was fastened by dog clips. The handrail was cut back to end on the side of the smokebox and a horizontal rail was put on the door. Note this engine had tablet apparatus on both sides of the tender, and the cab roof had been extended. The normal chimney was the Melton Constable "3rd Pattern" which was tall and tapered outwards to the top, with a rim and capuchon similar to Deeley's Midland type.

M&GN Class B - LNER Class D52 from 28/7/42.

(0)37

Sharp Stewart 3989.

To traffic 5/1894.

REPAIRS:
MC. ?/?—?/?/24.**G.**
Str. *by* 19/12/36. *Not repaired.*

BOILER:
37.

SHED:
Melton Constable *at* 1/10/36.

CONDEMNED: 3/2/37.
Cut up at Stratford.

038

Sharp Stewart 3990.

To traffic 5/1894.

REPAIRS:
MC. ?/?—?6/36.**G.**
Str. 30/9—17/12/37.**G.**
Str. 12/2—4/5/40.**G.**
Str. 15/8/43. *Not repaired.*

BOILER:
38.

SHED:
Melton Constable *at* 1/10/36.

RENUMBERED:
 038 17/12/37.
 2050 allocated.

CONDEMNED: 27/9/43.
Cut up at Stratford.

042

Sharp Stewart 3992.

To traffic 5/1894.

REPAIRS:
MC. ?/?—10/12/36.**G.**
Str. 31/3/40. *Not repaired.*

BOILER:
42.

SHED:
New England (M&GN)
at 1/10/36.

RENUMBERED:
042 10/12/36.

CONDEMNED: 28/6/40.
Cut up at Stratford.

043

Sharp Stewart 3993.

To traffic 5/1894.

REPAIRS:
Str. *by* 2/37—3/9/37.**G.**

BOILER:
43.

SHED:
Melton Constable *at* 1/10/36.

RENUMBERED:
043 3/9/37.

CONDEMNED: 1/6/43.
Cut up at Stratford.

047

Sharp Stewart 3997.

To traffic 6/1894.

REPAIRS:
MC. ?/?—?/6/36.**G.**
Str. 28/12/36—22/7/37.**G.**
Str. 27/9/39—30/1/40.**G.**
Str. 4/5/42. *Not repaired.*
Damaged in air raid at Norwich
28/4/42.

BOILER:
47.

SHED:
Melton Constable *at* 1/10/36.

RENUMBERED:
047 22/7/37.

CONDEMNED: 13/6/42.
Cut up at Stratford.

(0)48

Sharp Stewart 3998.

To traffic 7/1894.

REPAIRS:
MC. ?/?—?/?/22.**G.**

BOILER:
48.

SHEDS:
Melton Constable *at* 1/10/36.
New England (M&GN) 20/1/37.

CONDEMNED: 18/11/37.
Cut up at Stratford.

01

Sharp Stewart 4001.

To traffic 8/1894.

REPAIRS:
MC. ?/?—?/?/25.**G.**
MC. ?/?—?/10/36.**?.**
Str. ?/9/37. *Not repaired.*

BOILER:
1.

SHED:
Yarmouth Beach *at* 1/10/36.

RENUMBERED:
01 20/10/36.

CONDEMNED: 12/11/37.
Cut up at Stratford.

(0)3

Sharp Stewart 4003.

To traffic 8/1894.

REPAIRS:
MC. ?/?—?/?/25.**G.**
Str. *by* 4/37. *Not repaired.*

BOILER:
3.

SHEDS:
Yarmouth Beach *at* 1/10/36.
Peterborough East 29/12/36.
New England (M&GN) 11/1/37.

CONDEMNED: 3/6/37.
Cut up at Stratford.

(0)4

Sharp Stewart 4004.

To traffic 8/1894.

REPAIRS:
MC. ?/?—?/?/23.**G.**

BOILER:
4.

SHED:
Melton Constable *at* 1/10/36.

CONDEMNED: 3/2/38.
Cut up at Stratford.

05

Sharp Stewart 4005.

To traffic 8/1894.

REPAIRS:
MC. ?/?—?/?/25.**G.**

BOILER:
5.

SHEDS:
Melton Constable *at* 1/10/36.
South Lynn 28/12/36.

RENUMBERED:
05 ?/11/36.

CONDEMNED: 20/7/37.
Cut up at Stratford.

07

Sharp Stewart 4007.

To traffic 8/1894.

REPAIRS:
MC. ?/?—?/?/23.**G.**
MC. ?/?—22/10/36.**G.**

BOILER:
7.

SHED:
South Lynn *at* 1/10/36.

RENUMBERED:
07 22/10/36.

CONDEMNED: 8/6/37.
Cut up at Stratford.

011

Sharp Stewart 4008.

To traffic 9/1894.

REPAIRS:
MC. ?/?—?/7/36.**?.**
Str. 27/2—16/9/37.**G.**
Str. 17/3—13/5/39.**L.**
Str. 1/12/39—9/1/40.**?.**
Str. 28/2—12/4/40.**?.**
Str. 4/8/42. *Not repaired.*

BOILER:
11.

SHEDS:
Peterborough East *at* 1/10/36.
New England (M&GN) 3/2/37.
Peterborough East 10/6/38.
New England (M&GN) 30/4/39.

RENUMBERED:
011 16/9/37.

CONDEMNED: 29/8/42.
Cut up at Stratford.

012

Sharp Stewart 4009.

To traffic 11/1894.

REPAIRS:
Str. ?/?—22/11/37.**G.**
Str. ?/?—28/6/40.**G.**

BOILER:
12.

SHEDS:
Yarmouth Beach *at* 1/10/36.
Melton Constable 24/7/37.

RENUMBERED:
012 22/11/37.

CONDEMNED: 18/8/42.
Cut up at Stratford.

013

Sharp Stewart 4010.

To traffic 11/1894.

REPAIRS:
MC. ?/?—?/4/34.**G.**
Str. 19/12/36—18/5/37.**G.**
Str. 27/1—15/2/41.**G.**
Str. 30/7/41. *Not repaired.*

BOILERS:
13.
18 *(ex18)* 18/5/37.

SHED:
New England (M&GN)
at 1/10/36.

RENUMBERED:
013 18/5/37.

CONDEMNED: 6/9/41.
Cut up at Stratford.

(0)14

Sharp Stewart 4011.

To traffic 11/1894.

REPAIRS:
MC. ?/?—?/?/26.**G.**
Str. *by* 19/12/36. *Not repaired.*

BOILER:
14.

SHED:
Melton Constable *at* 1/10/36.

CONDEMNED: 6/2/37.
Cut up at Stratford.

(0)17

Sharp Stewart 4012.

To traffic 11/1894.

REPAIRS:
MC. ?/?—?/?/26.**G.**

BOILER:
17.

SHED:
Melton Constable *at* 1/10/36.

CONDEMNED: 14/10/37.
Cut up at Stratford.

(0)18

Sharp Stewart 4013.

To traffic 11/1894.

REPAIRS:
MC. ?/?—?/?/23.**G.**
Str. *by* 19/12/36. *Not repaired.*

BOILER:
18.

SHED:
South Lynn *at* 1/10/36.

CONDEMNED: 6/2/37.
Cut up at Stratford.

(0)74

Beyer, Peacock 4066.

To traffic 10/1899.

REPAIRS:
MC. ?/?—?/?/18.**G.**
Str. *by* 4/37. *Not repaired.*

BOILER:
74.

SHED:
South Lynn *at* 1/10/36.

CONDEMNED: 21/5/37.
Cut up at Stratford.

(0)75

Beyer, Peacock 4067.

To traffic 10/1899.

REPAIRS:
MC. ?/?—?/?/16.**G.**

BOILER:
75.

SHED:
South Lynn *at* 1/10/36.

CONDEMNED: 6/2/37.
Cut up at Stratford.

076

Beyer, Peacock 4068.

To traffic 10/1899.

REPAIRS:
MC. ?/?—?/1/36.**?.**
Str. 23/8—11/11/37.**G.**
Str. 18/9—11/12/40.**G.**
Str. 10/7—2/8/41.**L.**
Str. 19/6/43. *Not repaired.*

BOILERS:
76.
13 *(ex13)* 11/11/37.

SHEDS:
New England *at* 1/10/36.
Peterborough East 23/11/37.
New England (M&GN) 30/4/39.
South Lynn 28/4/43.

RENUMBERED:
 076 11/11/37.
2051 allocated.

CONDEMNED: 17/7/43.

Cut up at Stratford.

078

Beyer, Peacock 4070.

To traffic 11/1899.

REPAIRS:
MC. ?/?—?/?23.**G.**
MC. ?/?—?/11/36.**?.**

BOILER:
78.

SHED:
South Lynn *at* 1/10/36.

RENUMBERED:
078 ?/11/36.

CONDEMNED: 16/2/38.
Cut up at Stratford.

079

Beyer, Peacock 4071.

To traffic 11/1899.

REPAIRS:
MC. ?/?—?/?/17.**G.**
MC. ?/?—?/11/36.**?.**
Str. ?/12/36. *Not repaired.*

BOILER:
79.

SHED:
Peterborough East *at* 1/10/36.

RENUMBERED:
079 ?/11/36.

CONDEMNED: 3/2/37.
Cut up at Stratford.

(0)80

Beyer, Peacock 4072.

To traffic 11/1899.

REPAIRS:
MC. ?/?—?/?/19.**G.**

BOILER:
80.

SHED:
Melton Constable *at* 1/10/36.

CONDEMNED: 9/2/37.
Cut up at Stratford.

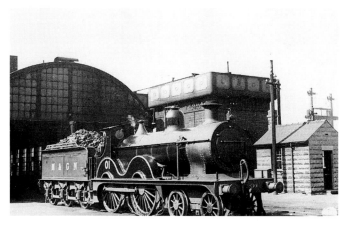

In 1935/36 seven of the class, Nos.1, 4, 12, 38, 42, 48 and 78 were fitted with a shorter, wider, tapered chimney with capuchon. Eleven are known to have had the cab roof extended: Nos.4, 5, 7, 11, 14, 17, 38, 42, 48, 76 and 78.

Six, Nos.01, 012, 013,0 43, 047 and 079 are known to have retained the short cab roof and it is very probable this also applied to the other six, Nos.3, 18, 37, 74, 75 and 80, none of which got LNER number or any repairs.

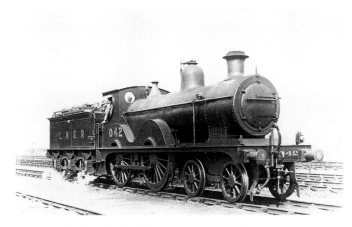

Whilst capuchon was normally retained, at least No.076 ran in LNER days without one. No.78 had lost its capuchon by 1935 before it got a short, wide chimney.

Most of the class did not have any carriage heater connection at the front end although the M&GN had fitted Nos.12, 38, 76 and 78 by the take-over date. These engines had the heater connection and hose on the right side of the engine.

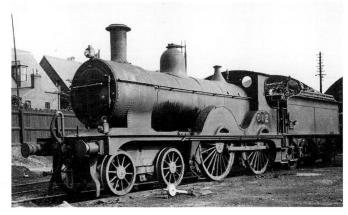

The short, wide chimney did not prove much better and at least two, Nos.12 and 38 reverted to tall chimney of the type without capuchon.

On those fitted by the M&GN the heater pipe was outside the running plate angle to just ahead of the coupled wheel and then passed to the inside.

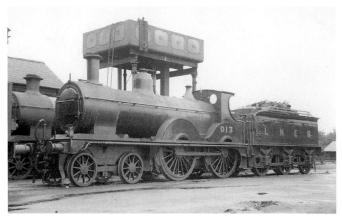

Those repaired by the LNER were given a front end heater connection and the piping was outside for the full length of the running plate, on the left hand side with the hose also on the opposite, right, side of the coupling hook.

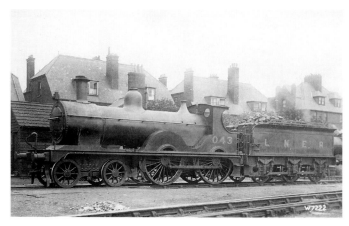

When No.043 was ex Stratford after general repair on 3rd September 1937, they had used 12in. numbers but to accommodate them they had removed the beading. It was the only one so treated.

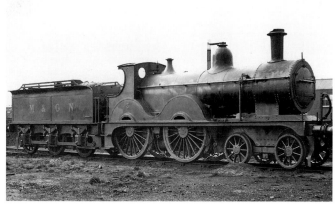

Until late M&GN days sanding was steam applied ahead of the leading coupled wheels, and some had a box on the front of the tender for gravity application to aid running in reverse. From the mid-1930s steam sanding behind the leading coupled wheels was added to some, but not all, in place of that on the tender.

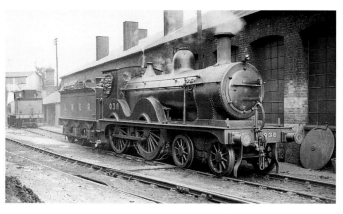

During 1937 six others - 013 (May); 047 (July); 011 (September); 012 and 076 (November); and 038 (December), had a general repair at Stratford but all retained the splasher beading because only 10in. transfers were used to fit inside the beading. All had combined steam and vacuum brake valve in which the small ejector had to act as blower, but at the 1937 general repairs, Stratford put separate blower on Nos.011, 012, 013, 038, 043. Nos.047 and 076 would probably also be so fitted.

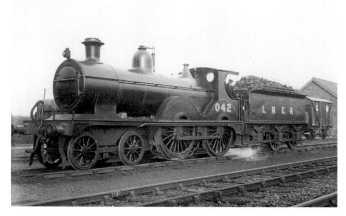

Where Melton Constable applied the transfers for number and LNER, they left the splasher beading in place although the 12in. numbers overlapped it.

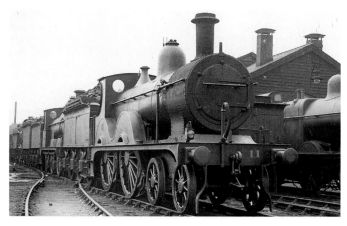

Buffers had hollow spindles, parallel shanks and square flanges with thick wood packing between them and the beam. All were alike, and no variation was seen or recorded.

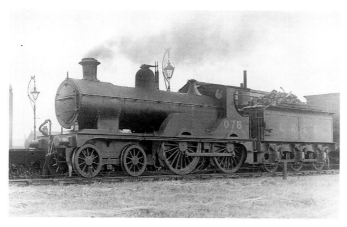

In 1935, when No.78 was fitted with a shorter wider chimney, its blast pipe had a jumper top put on and the smokebox was extended even further forward, but it was the only one so done, and the jumper top proved prone to jamming. Had this engine not been withdrawn on 16th February 1938 without getting any attention at Stratford it would probably have reverted to tall chimney as did Nos.12 and 38.

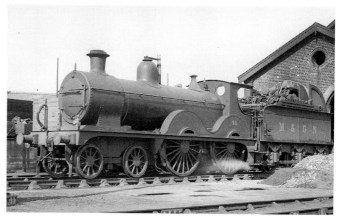

From 1928 the M&GN adopted the 14in. LMS style of tender lettering, but continued the use of brass numbers on the splasher which formed part of the cab side, but the armorial was discarded from the leading splasher. All D52 class were in this style when the LNER took them over.

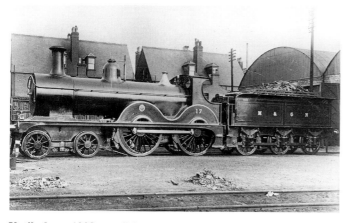

Until about 1928, small letters were used on the tender and the company's armorial was on the front splasher.

Ten of the class, Nos.3, 4, 14, 17, 18, 37, 48, 74, 75 and 80, never received any LNER numbering or lettering and had final M&GN livery when cut up at Stratford. Five were withdrawn in February 1937, four more by November and then No.4 on 3rd February 1938.

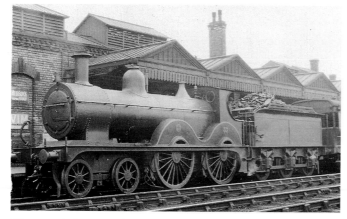

The use of the armorial survived the change of smokebox door (which was completed in 1931) but none reached LNER days.

With a show of initiative Melton Constable put LNER numbering on engine 01 on 20th October 1936 and on to 079 in November. Both retained M&GN on the tender, and although the new number was put on the buffer beam it was in M&GN style with serifs.

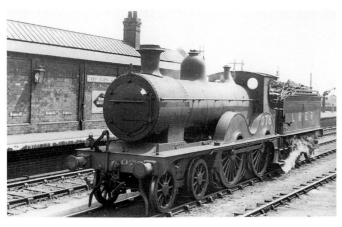

In this same style on the engine, Melton changed Nos.07, 042 and 078 between 22nd October 1936 and 10th December 1936, but the tender was altered to LNER.

The seven further re-numberings were done during general repairs at Stratford in 1937 and all got the standard 4½in. numerals on the buffer beam. They were: 013 (18th May), 047 (22nd July), 043 (3rd September), 011 (16th September), 076 (11th November), 012 (22nd November) and 038 (17th December). Here, 14th March 1939, No.012 is at Melton Constable on a Class D goods.

D 53 Class

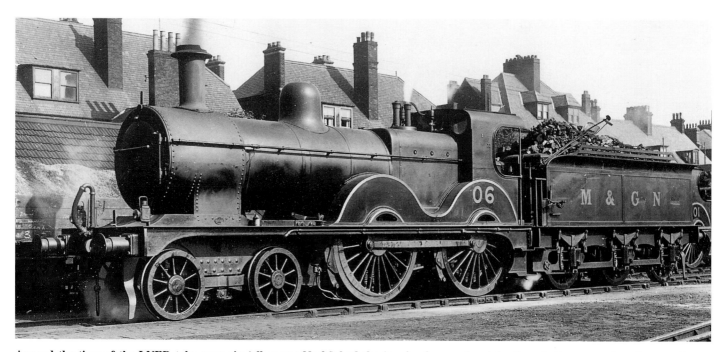

Around the time of the LNER take-over, six (all except No.36) had the 'pop' valves replaced by Ramsbottom open type because it was claimed 'pop' type startled farm stock near the line. Between November 1936 and January 1937 Melton Constable took the brass numbers from 2, 6 and 50, putting 12in. painted and unshaded numbers on, but leaving M&GN on the tender.

Early in 1937 No.02 went to Stratford for general repair and it did not then have front end heater connection nor separate blower control.

M&GN Class C - LNER Class D53 from 28/7/42

(0)36

Sharp Stewart 3988.

To traffic 5/1894.

REPAIRS:
MC. ?/?—?/5/29.**G**.
Rebuilt to Class C.

BOILER:
36.

SHED:
Peterborough East *at* 1/10/36.

CONDEMNED: 4/1/37.
Cut up at Stratford.

044

Sharp Stewart 3994.

To traffic 6/1894.

REPAIRS:
MC. ?/?—?/5/30.**G**.
Rebuilt to Class C.
MC. ?/?—?/7/35.**G**.
Str. 15/12/36—3/7/37.**G**.
Str. 13/5/41. *Not repaired.*

BOILER:
44.

SHEDS:
Peterborough East *at* 1/10/36.
New England (M&GN) 29/9/38.

RENUMBERED:
044 3/7/37.

CONDEMNED: 15/8/41.
Cut up at Stratford.

049

Sharp Stewart 3999.

To traffic 7/1894.

REPAIRS:
MC. ?/?—?/2/31.**G**.
Rebuilt to Class C.
MC. ?/?—?/11/35.**G**.
Str. 18/2—30/10/37.**G**.
Str. 20/8/41. *Not repaired.*

BOILER:
49.

SHEDS:
New England (M&GN)
at 1/10/36.
Peterborough East 30/11/37.
New England (M&GN) 30/4/39.

RENUMBERED:
049 30/10/37.

CONDEMNED: 11/9/41.
Cut up at Stratford.

050

Sharp Stewart 4000.

To traffic 7/1894.

REPAIRS:
MC. ?/?—?/11/29.**G**.
Rebuilt to Class C.
Str. *by* 2/37—1/9/37.**G**.
Str. ?/?—8/1/41.**G**.

BOILERS:
50.
  2 *(ex02)* 1/9/37.
36 *(ex02)* 8/1/41.

SHEDS:
Peterborough East *at* 1/10/36.
New England (M&GN) 18/4/39.
Yarmouth Beach 28/4/43.

RENUMBERED:
  050 11/36.
2052 allocated.

CONDEMNED: 25/1/45.
Cut up at Stratford.

02

Sharp Stewart 4002.

To traffic 8/1894.

REPAIRS:
MC. ?/?—?/4/31.**G**.
Rebuilt to Class C.
Str. ?/?—?/8/37.**G**.
Str. ?/?—?/2/40.**G**.

BOILERS:
  2.

36 *(ex36)* ?/8/37.
  6 *(ex06)* ?/2/40.

SHEDS:
Melton Constable *at* 1/10/36.
Yarmouth Beach 17/4/40.

RENUMBERED:
02 ?/1/37.

CONDEMNED: 19/5/43.
Cut up at Stratford.

06

Sharp Stewart 4006.

To traffic 8/1894.

REPAIRS:
MC. ?/?—?/8/30.**G**.
Rebuilt to Class C.
MC. ?/?—?/11/35.**G**.
Str. 29/5—19/10/37.**G**.
Str. 28/7—12/8/38.**L**.
Str. 31/5—13/7/40.**H**.
Str. 13/1—8/3/41.**G**.
Str. 27/2/44. *Not repaired.*

BOILERS:
  6.
50 *(ex050)* 19/10/37.
77 *(ex077)* 8/3/41.

SHED:
Yarmouth Beach *at* 1/10/36.

RENUMBERED:
  06 11/36.
2053 allocated.

CONDEMNED: 22/3/44.
Cut up at Stratford.

077

Beyer, Peacock 4069.

To traffic 11/1899.

REPAIRS:
MC. ?/?—?/12/30.**G**.
Rebuilt to Class C.
Str. *by* 2/37—29/10/37.**G**.
Str. ?/?—15/2/41.**G**.

BOILERS:
77.
  2 *(ex02)* 15/2/41.

SHEDS:
New England (M&GN)
at 1/10/36.
Peterborough East 5/11/37.
New England (M&GN) 30/4/39.
Melton Constable 28/4/43.
Yarmouth Beach 25/7/43.

RENUMBERED:
077 29/10/37.
2054 allocated.

CONDEMNED: 22/1/45.
Cut up at Stratford.

WORKS CODES:- Cw - Cowlairs. Dar- Darlington. Dfu - Dunfermline shed. Don - Doncaster. Ghd - Gateshead. Gor - Gorton. MC - Melton Constable. Inv - Inverurie. Str - Stratford.
REPAIR CODES:- **C/H** - Casual Heavy. **C/L** - Casual Light. **G** - General. **H**- Heavy. **H/I** - Heavy Intermediate. **L** - Light. **L/I** - Light Intermediate. **N/C** - Non-Classified.

Ex Stratford in August 1937, No.02 had four changes in detail. It got the boiler from No.36 (which had not been changed to Ramsbottom safety valves), a separate blower control was put on, front end connection for carriage heating was fitted, and it got LNER style numbers and letters. Whilst the latter were the standard 12in., only 10in. transfers were used on the splasher so that the beading could be retained. The other five engines also got 10in. numbers put on by Stratford at repairs from July to October 1937 at which they too had separate blower control fitted.

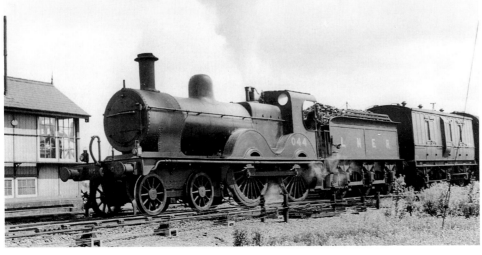

(above) Where front end connection for heating was added by the M&GN (No.49 got it in November 1935) the pipe was outside the angle of the running plate to just ahead of the leading coupled wheel. It then crossed over to the inside and the connection was on the off side of the drawhook. In late 1935 Nos.6 and 77 had front connection put on at Melton.

(left) In 1937 Nos.02 (August), 044 (July), and 050 (September) had front heater connection added by Stratford and, on them, the pipe ran the full length of the engine to cross over behind the buffer beam.

Unless there were wartime additions, which were not recorded, No.077 - in M&GN days - was the only one to have steam sanding added to the rear of the leading coupled wheels.

(right) Ex Stratford 1st September 1937 from a general repair, No.050 did not have the extra sanding added for reverse running.

(below) No.36 was withdrawn 4th January 1937 and received no LNER attention, it also escaped the change to Ramsbottom safety valves, but its boiler, still with 'pop' valves, then provided a spare for the class. It served No.02 from August 1937 to February 1940 and No.050 from 8th January 1941 to 25th January 1945 withdrawal.

From around 1930 all the Class C Rebuilds had the Johnson type smokebox door replaced by the later Midland type without central fastening and secured by six dog clips equally spaced around the rim. The handrail was cut to finish on the side of the smokebox and a cross rail was fitted to the door. Note that the splasher cut-outs were not put into the wider splashers whereas the rebuilds with small boiler kept them.

In line with Deeley's ideas, the earlier boilers carried a single lock-up safety valve behind the two Ramsbottoms but the lock-up had gone by the early 1930's. Note change to chocolate coloured paint and use of 1928 LMS style of tender lettering but retention of armorial.

By August 1933, three, Nos.45, 55 and 56 had been fitted with a Stanier type tapered stovepipe chimney, jumper top to the blastpipe and a further extension to the smokebox. Nos.45 and 55 kept this chimney to withdrawal. Note that splashers had again been given openings; all ten were so treated.

M&GN Class C Rebuilt - LNER Class D54 from 28/7/42

(0)39

Sharp Stewart 3991.

To traffic 5/1894.

REPAIRS:
MC. ?/?—?/08.**G**. *Rebuilt with Type H boiler.*
MC. ?/?—?/1/24.**G**. *Rebuilt.*
Str. *by* 19/12/36. *Not repaired.*

BOILER:
39.

SHED:
Melton Constable *at* 1/10/36.

CONDEMNED: 6/2/37.
Cut up at Stratford.

(0)45

Sharp Stewart 3995.

To traffic 6/1894.

REPAIRS:
MC. ?/?—?/?/09.**G**. *Rebuilt.*
MC. ?/?—?/?/26.**G**.
Str. *by* 19/12/36. *Not repaired.*

BOILER:
45.

SHED:
South Lynn *at* 1/10/36.

CONDEMNED: 4/1/37.
Cut up at Stratford.

046

Sharp Stewart 3996.

To traffic 6/1894.

REPAIRS:
MC. ?/?—?/?/16.**G**. *Rebuilt.*
Str. ?/?—10/12/37.**G**.
Str. ?/?—2/3/40.**G**.

BOILERS:
46.
56 *(ex056)* 10/12/37.

SHEDS:
Yarmouth Beach *at* 1/10/36.
South Lynn 23/2/37.

RENUMBERED:
046 ?/3/37.

CONDEMNED: 31/3/43.
Cut up at Stratford.

051

Sharp Stewart 4190.

To traffic 8/1896.

REPAIRS:
MC. ?/?—?/?/16.**G**. *Rebuilt.*
MC. ?/?—?/7/35.**G**.
Str. 10/4—3/9/37.**G**.
Heater connection at front.
Str. ?/3/38. *Weigh.*
Str. 22/11/39—6/4/40.**G**.
Str. 23/3/43. *Not repaired.*

BOILER:
51.

SHED:
South Lynn *at* 1/10/36.

RENUMBERED:
051 3/9/37.

CONDEMNED: 22/5/43.
Cut up at Stratford.

052

Sharp Stewart 4191.

To traffic 8/1896.

REPAIRS:
MC. ?/?—?/?/13.**G**. *Rebuilt.*
Str. *by* 2/37—22/8/37.**G**.
Str. ?/?—9/3/40.**G**.

BOILERS:
52.
54 *(ex054)* ?/8/37.

SHED:
South Lynn *at* 1/10/36.

RENUMBERED:
052 22/10/36.

CONDEMNED: 10/2/43.
Cut up at Stratford.

053

Sharp Stewart 4192.

To traffic 8/1896.

REPAIRS:
MC. ?/?—?/?/10.**G**. *Rebuilt.*

MC. ?/?—?/7/35.**G**.
Str. 17/3—17/7/37.**G**.
Str. 30/9/39. *Not repaired.*

BOILER:
53.

SHEDS:
South Lynn *at* 1/10/36.
Melton Constable 17/11/37.
South Lynn 22/1/38.

RENUMBERED:
053 *by* 2/37.

CONDEMNED: 29/1/40.
Cut up at Stratford.

054

Sharp Stewart 4193.

To traffic 9/1896.

REPAIRS:
MC. ?/?—?/?/14.**G**. *Rebuilt.*
MC. ?/?—22/10/36.**?**.
Str. *by* 2/37—15/5/37.**G**.

BOILERS:
54.
39 *(ex39)* 15/5/37.

SHED:
Melton Constable *at* 1/10/36.

RENUMBERED:
054 22/10/36.

CONDEMNED: 20/10/39.
Cut up at Stratford.

055

Sharp Stewart 4194.

To traffic 9/1896.

REPAIRS:
MC. ?/?—?/08.**G**. *Rebuilt with Type H boiler.*
MC. ?/?—?/7/25.**G**. *Rebuilt.*
MC. ?/?—?/5/36.**H**.
Str. 17/12/36—8/4/37.**G**.
Front end heater connection.
Str. 5/5—22/7/39.**G**.
Str. 13/5—30/7/40.**G**.
Str. 18/10—2/11/40.**L**.
Str. 10/10/43. *Not repaired.*

BOILER:
55.

SHEDS:
South Lynn *at* 1/10/36.
Yarmouth Beach 17/11/37.
Melton Constable 7/5/42.

RENUMBERED:
055 8/4/37.
2055 allocated.

CONDEMNED: 5/11/43.
Cut up at Stratford.

056

Sharp Stewart 4195.

To traffic 9/1896.

REPAIRS:
MC. ?/?—?/?/12.**G**. *Rebuilt.*
Str. *by* 2/37—24/9/37.**G**.
Str. ?/?—26/4/40.**G**.

BOILERS:
56.
57 *(ex57)* 24/9/37.

SHEDS:
Yarmouth Beach *at* 1/10/36.
Melton Constable 18/7/43.

RENUMBERED:
056 *by* 2/37.
2056 allocated.

CONDEMNED: 4/11/43.
Cut up at Stratford.

(0)57

Sharp Stewart 4196.

To traffic 9/1896.

REPAIRS:
MC. ?/?—?/?/12.**G**. *Rebuilt.*
MC. ?/?—?/?/30.**G**.

BOILERS:
57.
57 *(new)* ?/?/30.

SHED:
South Lynn *at* 1/10/36.

CONDEMNED: 6/2/37.
Cut up at Stratford.

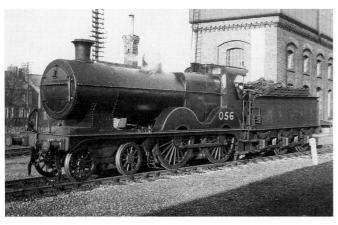

Late in 1936, No.056 had its stovepipe replaced by a short wide chimney which had a plain rim and no capuchon. Its brass numbers were taken off and Melton Constable put on 056 in 12in. painted and unshaded figures leaving M&GN on the tender. They also changed the buffer beam number to 056 but in their style with serifs. No.056 is believed to have retained this chimney to withdrawal.

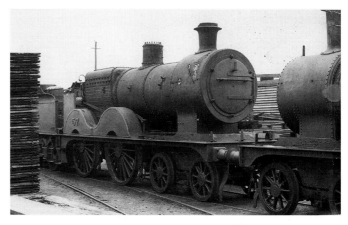

No.57 still had a tall chimney but without a capuchon in 1935, although sometime in 1936 this had been changed by Melton Constable to the short, wide type with capuchon. It was one of the engines which the LNER decided as not worth repairing and so was withdrawn on 6th February 1937, but the boiler - new in 1930 - was then used by No.056 from 24th September to withdrawal in 1943.

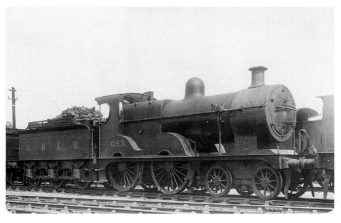

The normal chimney was Deeley type with capuchon but some had the capuchon taken off, probably due to corrosion. No.053 had been so treated when ex works at Stratford on 17th July 1937.

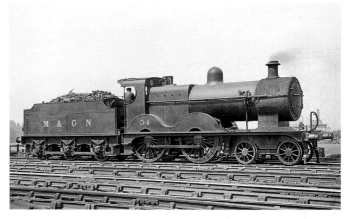

From about 1930 some new replacement boilers were supplied from Derby. Instead of the small ejector being on the firebox backplate, it was now alongside the large one on the side of the boiler. None of D54 class got separate blower control. These newer boilers had four small washout plugs on each side of the firebox instead of two large ones on each shoulder. They also had Ross 'pop' safety valves which the M&GN replaced later with Ramsbottom type.

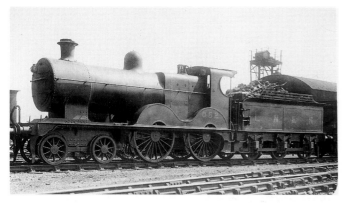

No.052 retained tall chimney with capuchon until it went to Stratford in February 1937. When ex works in August it had been fitted with a short, wide chimney, most probably taken from No.57 which had been scrapped earlier that year.

After 1937 only three of the older boilers remained in service. No.054 had the 1924 built one from No.39 after the latter was withdrawn in February 1937, No.054 kept that boiler, with two plugs on each shoulder and small ejector in the cab, to its withdrawal in October 1939. No.053 carried one to its January 1940 withdrawal but with the small ejector moved from the cab to alongside the large one on the boiler side. The third one, put on No.055 in July 1925 remained unaltered and was with that engine to its withdrawal as the last of the class on 5th November 1943.

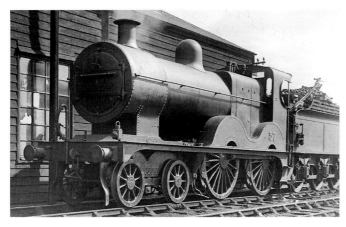

As the most powerful passenger class possessed by the M&GN they were not intended for working any trains tender first. In consequence, none had carriage heater connection fitted at the front end when the LNER took them over. The three withdrawn in early 1937, Nos.39, 45 and 57, were left unchanged.

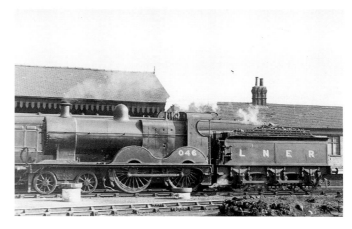

Another indication that this class was not intended to work trains tender first was that none were fitted with sanding to the rear of the coupled wheels.

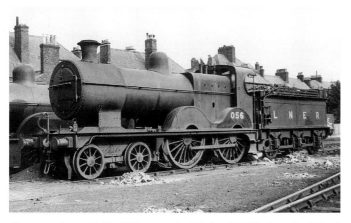

Commencing with No.055, ex works 8th April 1937, Stratford fitted the other seven with front heater connection, using the LNER style with the pipe outside the angle iron for the full length of the engine.

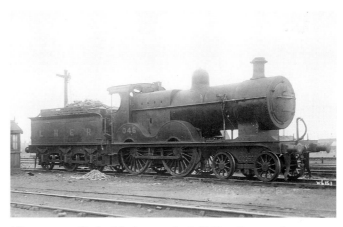

All were provided with the standard 2950 gallons tender as used by Classes D52 and D53, but when the larger boiler was put on, an extra coal rail was added. The rails always remained open type.

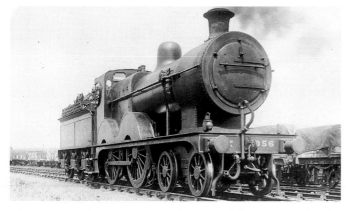

After the front heater connection was fitted, it was usual for the hose to be carried. Note the chain to prevent it swinging loose. During summer periods when carriage heating was not provided, some had the connecting hose taken off and left at the shed.

Only one change of tender was made. In July 1936 the tender from scrapped Class A 4-4-0 No.22 was put with No.54 which kept it to withdrawal in 1939. This flush-sided 3000 gallon tender had been built about 1924 for No.22.

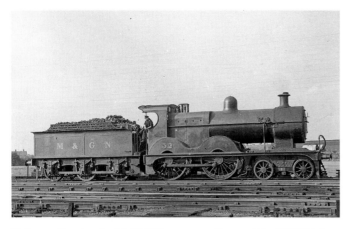

This was the standard M&GN passenger livery at the LNER take-over, brown paint with a very limited amount of lining. Nos.39, 45 and 57 had this painting when withdrawn.

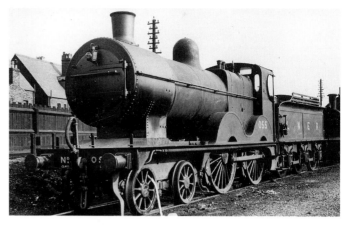

Between 8th April (No.055) and 10th December 1937 (No.046) Stratford put black paint with single red lining on to Nos.046, 051, 052, 053, 054, 055 and 056. 12in. letters were used on the tender but only 10in. numbers on the splasher so that they could be put inside the brass beading. No.055 was ex works from another general repair on 22nd July 1939 at which it acquired classification on the buffer beam. This was C/3 because LNER Class D54 was only introduced in July 1942 and is unlikely to have been carried by any of the five then surviving.

On 22nd October 1936 Melton Constable removed the brass numerals from Nos.52 and 54, replacing them with 12in. painted and unshaded numbers but leaving the M&GN on the tender. Before sending Nos.53 and 56 to Stratford in February 1937 Melton re-numbered them in the same style.

The main use of this class was on the through express trains from Yarmouth Beach to and from the Midlands on which the engines worked as far west as Nottingham and Leicester. Here No.53 is approaching Nottingham (Midland) on a through train to Manchester which ran in the summer seasons.

No.052 was at Stratford by February 1937, but escaped the wholesale scrapping of M&GN locos but it was August 1937 before leaving works with the boiler taken off No.054.

No.57 had its final repair at Melton Constable works as seen here on 1st July 1936. It was an early victim of the LNER take-over as it was withdrawn on 6th February 1937 without getting its LNER number or initials.